A VIEW FROM
THE TOP

*Avon's elite leaders share their stories
and strategies to succeed*

Foreword by Sheri McCoy

THRIVE Publishing
A Division of PowerDynamics Publishing, Inc.
San Francisco, California
www.thrivebooks.com

ISBN: 978-0-9897129-4-1

Library of Congress Control Number: 2014960267

Printed in the United States of America on acid-free paper.

We dedicate this book to you...

our reader; the Avon® representative, the direct seller, the entrepreneur, whether you are experienced or just getting started. You recognize the power of learning from others who have accomplished what you seek to achieve. We salute you for embracing knowledge and allowing our stories and success strategies to enhance your life and advance your career. We celebrate your commitment to being the best you can be!

The Co-Authors of *A View From The Top Volume 3:*
Avon's elite leaders share their stories
and strategies to succeed

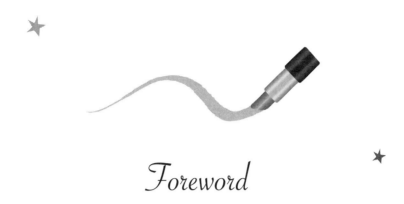

Foreword

It is an honor to lead this great company—a company that is committed to helping women build better lives for themselves and their families. Avon® has a powerful and iconic brand that people around the world love. We have terrific products. Most important, we have the Avon representatives who have built and sustained our business for over 125 years.

The stories in this book reflect the heart and soul of Avon. In reading them you will see the strength of our business model and how it can provide financial freedom. You will find inspiration in the personal stories of victories and setbacks. And, like me, I know that you will be truly impressed by the hard work and dedication each person has put into building their Avon business.

The power of Avon has always been in how the Avon ladies (and a few good men) tap into their social circles to spread the word about Avon's products and mentor and support one another as members of the Avon family. I congratulate each person in this book for continuing Avon's great tradition.

Sheri McCoy
Chief Executive Officer, Avon Products, Inc.

Table of Contents

Acknowledgements

An important element for succeeding in business is gratitude. We would like to express ours here, to those who have turned our vision for this book into a reality.

This book is the brilliant concept of Lisa Wilber, who shared her story in the first volume of *A View from the Top*. She realized how valuable our collective knowledge and experiences would be to those who truly strive to succeed in their businesses. The result was putting our ideas into a second, and now a third, comprehensive book to share our stories and strategies. The first two books were so well received, and helped so many people, that Lisa put the wheels in motion for this third volume. We are grateful for Lisa's vision.

Caterina Rando is the founder of Thrive Publishing and a respected business strategist and speaker. Without Caterina's "take action" spirit, her positive attitude and her commitment to excellence, you would not be reading this book of which we are all so proud. She was supported by a dedicated team who worked diligently to put together the best possible book for you. We are truly grateful for everyone's stellar contribution.

To Karen Gargiulo, who served as project manager and copyeditor for this book, we appreciate your patient guidance and the expertise you shared to ensure that this book would be the best it could be.

To Noël Voskuil and Tammy Tribble, our designers extraordinaire, who brought their creative talents to the cover and book layout, thank you both for your enthusiasm, problem solving and attention to detail throughout this project.

To Monique Cabading and Rua Necaise, who provided us with keen proofreading eyes, thank you for your support and contribution and for making us read so perfectly on paper.

The Co-Authors of *A View From the Top Volume 3:*
Avon's elite leaders share their stories
and strategies to succeed

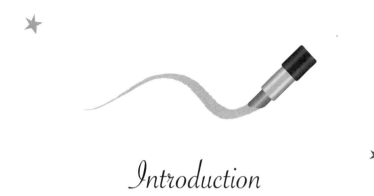

Introduction

Thirty-three years ago I wrote to Avon® Products, Inc., from Guam and asked to become a representative. I was 18 years old and a newly married Navy wife. I had worked since I was 13—picking tobacco during the summer and later working as a waitress at the local ice cream parlor. During high school, I was enrolled in a program called "co-op," where I was released early from school to work in an office in my town. I barely remember a time when I did not have my own money to spend or to save for something I wanted.

When I arrived on Guam in March 1981, finding a way to earn my own money was a top priority. The wives in my husband's command were all older than I was, many of them much older. Most of them did not work and did activities together so that they would not feel so alone while their husbands were working. Among the activities that were common were home parties. I went to quite a few and then hosted some of my own, earning many free items. I remember wanting to earn a particularly nice picnic set with all the pieces from a Tupperware® party—and I earned it. I saw a lot of different companies doing business on Guam, yet I had not run across an Avon representative. I wrote to the company and asked if I could sell on Guam. They told me I just needed to send them $30 and they would send me a starter kit.

That is how my story of starting in direct sales began. As I was building my Avon business over the years and met so many of Avon's top performers, I thought to myself, "Wouldn't it be great if there were a book with chapters written by the top leaders? A new or seasoned representative could learn about how inspiring all of these people are and the tips they have to share!"

I have found that some of the best projects start with the words, *Wouldn't it be great if…* and end with *Why don't I do it?* In the spring of 2012 the *A View from the Top* series was born. I had talked about this idea for many years. Most of the discussion was, "Why doesn't someone do a book?" It was not until 2012 that I suddenly realized that I was someone, too. Sometimes you just have to be the one to just do it. I contacted my Senior Executive Unit Leader (SEUL) friends, many of whom I had known for years and had seen at meetings and on the annual honors trips. I told them my idea and how I thought the book would make a big difference for so many people, and that sharing our stories and ideas would help inspire not only Avon representatives, but people in direct sales, too. Twenty-two SEULs jumped on board for the first book, followed in 2013 by another 25 SEULs for Volume 2, and you are holding Volume 3, with another 19 SEULs and Executive Unit Leaders (EULs).

Throughout the *A View from the Top* series of books, there are co-authors from just about every background imaginable. Many had humble beginnings and stumbled on direct sales as a way to improve their lives. Many chose direct sales as a part-time income and way to get out of the house and be with other adults, because they had small children. In this three-book series, Avon's very top representative leaders come from all walks of life, all ages and all backgrounds.

When you own this series of books, you hold in your hands the stories, ideas, and life experiences of 66 of Avon's top leaders. I find that truly remarkable and a dream come true. The best part is that these books will not grow stale! Our stories and ideas will be helpful to so many people in our industry for years to come.

> *"If we stop and look over the past and then into the future,*
> *we can see that the possibilities are growing greater and greater*
> *every day; that we have scarcely begun to reach the proper results*
> *from the field we have before us."*
> **—David H. McConnell, American founder of the**
> **California Perfume Company, later known as Avon Products, Inc.**

When David H. McConnell, a book salesman, started the California Perfume Company in 1886 (later known as Avon Products, Inc.), I wonder if he could have imagined how the direct sales profession would look today and how big a role his own company would play in this multi-billion dollar industry. Avon itself has annual sales over $10 billion and, since 1886, has changed the lives of millions and millions of people—primarily women. I have always loved the fact that Avon provided an opportunity for women to earn money and build a business before they were even allowed to vote! Our profession is full of stories of direct sales companies that have made a huge difference in so many lives.

One of the most talked about, life-altering experiences in direct sales is the ability to earn unlimited income, which includes the freedom to decide whether that means you want to earn some pocket money to help out with the expenses in your family or you want to build a direct sales empire of your own. I cannot think of many other professions that allow people to have those kinds of options and where it does not matter what race, gender or religion you are. It does not matter if you are young, old, or somewhere in between. It does not matter if you are short, tall, thin or bonus size. All that does matter is your willingness to set goals and to work hard toward their achievement.

For some, the direct sales profession is more than an income opportunity. It is a way to build lasting friendships that span decades, much like having an extended family. It is a way to have a support system. It is a profession where we can learn and grow together and be part of a bigger community.

The power in numbers is staggering when we get behind a cause we believe in. Within Avon, for example, there is the Avon Foundation. This organization was founded in 1955 and has grown to be the largest corporate-affiliated foundation that focuses on causes that impact women. It has raised and distributed over $957 million for causes such as breast cancer and domestic violence. Our profession is truly more than just a way to earn a living.

This brings me back to my story. After receiving my starter kit on Guam, I built a nice business there and earned my first President's Club award for personal sales. Since then, I have been divorced, remarried and divorced again. I have moved from Guam to Mississippi to South Carolina, and then to New Hampshire. I have lived in apartments and spent nearly 18 years living in a single-wide trailer in a trailer park. I built a new home and gave it to my now ex-husband as a parting gift when I released him to move on to another opportunity. I also built a new home that I live in right now with the daughter I adopted in 2005 when she was a newborn.

There have been so many changes in my life and one constant: my direct sales Avon business. Because of my business, I was able to earn over thirty all-expenses-paid trips to fabulous places like Ireland,

England, Hawaii, Alaska and the Mediterranean. I was able to decide to "release" my second husband and go on my own because I knew I had the income to support myself. I was given the opportunity to adopt my daughter, Lydia, as a 42-year-old single parent. I have friends all over the world and have the time and resources to do things like serve on the board of directors for The Academy of Multi-Level Marketing (TAMM) and run for the New Hampshire House of Representatives. My cumulative earnings passed $4 million this year for my leadership business. I am in awe of the power of this business to change the direction of my life. I did not have the typical education, skills nor background to create that type of income, yet with direct sales it has been possible.

*"You don't have to be great to start,
but you do have to start to be great."*
**—Zig Ziglar, American author, salesman
and motivational speaker**

My hope is that if you are reading these books, you are now realizing the greatness within you and that anything is possible. The 66 co-authors who wrote *A View from the Top* all started with a starter kit and a dream. We all had that first customer and that first team member who joined our business. We all had the disappointments that come with a non-paying customer or a big-talking new recruit who never makes a first order. The 66 of us never gave up and we want you to know that you shouldn't either.

Dream big! Decide that your goals and dreams are worth pursuing. Decide that you can make a difference for yourself and your family. Go after the top with a passion, knowing that your attitude is going to make a huge difference in your outcome. Along your journey, please know that we, the co-authors of *A View from the Top*, are with you every step of the way. Reread your favorite stories when you get discouraged. Highlight the ideas you are going to implement in your business. Reach out to the co-authors you relate to and connect with their social media pages or tap into their conference calls. Remember to share this resource with the leaders on your team as well. We want to make a difference in our profession and in the lives of direct sellers. We want to make a difference for you.

LISA M. WILBER
National Senior Executive Unit Leader

733 S. Stark Hwy., Weare, NH 03281
www.winnerinyou.com
www.facebook.com/winnerinyou

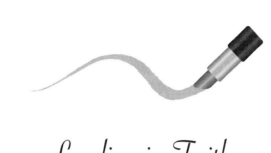

Leading in Faith

BY S. DIANE MELTON

I was born in Fairbanks, Alaska, at the Fort Wainwright Army Post hospital. My father, Larry Melton, Sr., was reassigned after serving four years in the U.S. Army there. So my parents, my older sister, Tonya, my two older brothers, Larry, Jr. and Gary, and I moved to Fort Jackson, South Carolina.

When my father was reassigned to Camp Casey, Korea, my mother, Annie Melton, did not want to continue relocating the entire family. She wanted my sister, brothers, and me to have a place to call home; therefore, we remained in South Carolina while my father went to Korea.

My dad served around the world and was away a lot during my childhood. Although he came home during the holidays and between tours, and made every attempt to parent remotely, we all sorely missed him. By the time he retired as a Command Sergeant Major, after serving thirty years, I was a junior in college.

Looking back, I respect and commend my mom for having such strength and confidence in her abilities to raise four children while my dad was away. She also worked full time for over thirty years at K-Mart®, working her way up to store manager. She was raised by her grandmother to be a humble, God-fearing woman of wonderful character and deep values. Thank you, great-grand-mother Gertrude Wilburn.

My mom made sure that I gained an understanding of hard work and the value of a dollar by having me earn my own money by age 16. For that I am grateful. I was a daddy's girl and must admit that I did not always recognize my mom's valuable wisdom. Thank God I know now. She is an amazing woman.

The Love of Learning

Although my mom and sister both married and created families, I took a different route. I became a serial student. I realized how much I loved to learn when I attended undergraduate school. I loved it so much that my parents told me that if I could get paid to go to school, I would make it a career.

After completing my undergraduate degree and earning an MBA, I worked in corporate sales and marketing for eight years. Then I had a major health scare. I had a biopsy and neck surgery to remove a lump in my neck. It was benign. However, I began to feel pain in my neck and arm and had an X-ray done. Doctors who viewed the X-ray told me I had a cyst on my spine and that if I had surgery, there was a chance I would be paralyzed. After months of prayer and several doctors' opinions, I learned that what was viewed on the X-ray was actually a piece of the X-ray equipment. The pain I was experiencing was rheumatoid arthritis.

After my distressing medical experience and plenty of self-reflection, I decided to pursue my dream of earning a PhD. I had already purchased my first home and had other financial obligations. I had to find a way to achieve my dream while being gainfully employed.

I earned my PhD from a non-traditional university while still working in corporate sales and marketing and eventually in higher education. Still, I felt the need for more. After much prayer and life circumstances, I relocated to Georgia while still teaching online. I did not know what my future would bring.

"For we walk by faith, not by sight."
—2 Corinthians 5:7, New King James Version

Choosing Avon

I was temporarily staying with Dr. Miles, my sister in Christ. I was not certain that I wanted to make Georgia my permanent residence, or what I wanted my next career move to be. I was at a crossroad in life and trusted in God.

"Some trust in chariots and some in horses,
but we trust in the name of the Lord our God."
—Psalm 20:7, New International version

In April 2011, I kept seeing Avon commercials on television. For some reason one night, each commercial resonated with me. I said aloud, "God, are you trying to tell me something?" I thought surely He did not want me to be an Avon representative. Even with three degrees, I was a woman who had self-doubt and needed to believe in herself again.

That night, I visited Avon's website. I discovered that everything Avon believed in—from the two causes the company supports to its dedication to empowering women—meant a lot to me. It felt like home.

I immediately contacted Avon through the Internet and expressed an interest in becoming a representative. I received a phone call from a district sales manager who had been with the company for more than thirty years. Through the phone, I felt her passion for, and belief in, Avon. As the song says, "She had me at hello."

An Amazing Lifestyle

My workday starts and ends based on the hours I set versus those created by a typical nine-to-five job. It is my business and the work I put in each day is for it's success. Having my own business motivates me to work harder than ever and is extremely rewarding. Unlike any other job I have had, Avon has afforded me the freedom and flexibility I need to be me and to embrace my heart's desires.

Through Avon, I have increased my income and earned trips to Las Vegas, Nevada and Orlando, Florida. The hotels, transportation and food were on Avon. While in Las Vegas, the top performers enjoyed a private Bon Jovi concert. There was not a bad seat in the house. It was a blast!

I also earned a beach trip, several prepaid Visa® gift cards, restaurant gift cards, group dinners, and other prizes based on incentives. In 2013, I bought my dream car of choice and even chose its color, make and model.

Spiritual Outlook

The Avon experience has increased my desire to leave a legacy and, through God's grace, to create generational wealth. More than ever, I listen for, lean toward, and trust in God's word wholeheartedly.

> *"Yet if anyone suffers as a Christian, let him not be ashamed,*
> *but let him glorify God in this matter."*
> **—1 Peter 4:16, New King James Version**

I thank God for every setback and challenge in life, which I believe are His ways of bringing me closer to Him. I do not look back, just forward. My ultimate goal in life is to please God.

> *"For we speak as messengers approved by God to be entrusted*
> *with the Good News. Our purpose is to please God, not people.*
> *He alone examines the motives of our hearts."*
> **—1: Thessalonians 2:4, New Living Testament**

Success in the Numbers

> *"…faith without works is dead…"*
> **—James 2:14-26, New King James Version**

Any success I have achieved has been by faith and God's grace.

- In 2013-2014, we had total team sales of $418,791.
- We ranked number one in total sales increase over the previous year for the Peachtree Division and for the second year in a row in our respective district.
- We were number one in the division for percentage order increase.
- For the second year in a row, we ranked number one in the division for team member growth. In 2012-2013, our increase in member growth was more than 361 percent.
- In 2013-2014, we had the second highest percentage increase in the division for the number of President's Club achievers—team members with personal sales of at least $10,100.

- We were the district recipients of the 2013-2014 Recruiting Excellence Award for "exemplifying the art of recruiting and mastery of commitment, actions and results."

Here are my proven strategies that led to these accomplishments. If you implement these, you can also achieve your dreams.

Know your *why*. Write down *why* you joined Avon. Keep your why top of mind to stay focused through the highs and lows you are sure to experience along the way.

Have goals. Write down stretch goals with achievement dates. You may create stretch goals and triumphant dates that seem unachievable. However, if you believe, trust in the Lord, and *work hard,* anything is possible.

Create a plan. Write down your plan for achieving your goals. I created a growth-strategy plan to expand my market. This increased sales revenue and active team members. Do not be afraid to re-evaluate your plan and make adjustments.

Invest time. Treat your business like a business. Develop a daily/weekly work schedule solely for your Avon business. Do not waiver from it unless absolutely necessary. Share your work schedule with team members, customers, family and friends so they will learn to respect and honor your business and time.

Invest money. Be willing to invest your money in business essentials like supplies, tools, resources and events. Over time and through God's grace, your hard work will return that money three-fold.

Implement your plan. Execute your plan and analyze it along the way to ensure it is giving you a return. On the flipside, do not just throw in the towel if you see no immediate results. Discernment, persistence and patience are vital.

Develop your leadership style

"Leadership is a process whereby an individual influences a group of individuals to achieve a common goal."
—**Peter Northouse, author of *Leadership: Theory and Practice***

Know who you are as a leader. *Upward Mobility for Women Managers: Styles and Perceptions: Part 1,* an article written by Applebaum, Didus, Luongo, Shapiro, & Paz, published in 2013, discusses leadership styles. I am a self-proclaimed transformational leader. I have the ability to inspire, communicate, and set a clear vision. I am optimistic, enthusiastic, respectful, respected, truthful and experienced. These attributes influence individuals to join even when in doubt and to remain diligent even when things look bleak. In addition to being a transformational leader, I am a servant leader. I am passionate about serving and helping others work toward their dreams. Sometimes I have to change my leadership style based on the situation. This also makes me a situational leader.

Embrace diversity. Instill in your leaders the value that every individual brings, despite differences in age, ethnicity, educational level, socio-economic status, native tongue, disability or national origin. I have more than 200 team members from all over North America and other regions around the world, including Africa, Central America and the Caribbean. I make every attempt to capitalize on differences. Do not judge a book by its cover. Realize that some of your representatives can capture the attention of a target market that might not be able to relate to you. Recognize everyone's strengths and work with him or her to apply those strengths for the advancement of their business, which in turn, advances yours. It is a win-win arrangement. Work as a team toward creating generational wealth.

Keep past success in perspective. Avon acknowledges you for your performance, and rightly so—you work hard. Embrace your success and all of the accolades that come with it, and then move on. Do not get caught up in the celebrity of being successful. Keep your *why,* goal, and plan top of mind, and continue to press forward.

Recruit, train and stay connected. Be relentless about recruiting and looking for events like job fairs, conventions, trade shows, festivals, community/national events, storefronts, malls, industry expos, flea markets, senior communities, parking lot tailgates, and church and school events. If you are allowed to set up, be there and ready to participate. Be diligent, because team members will quit for various reasons. While recruiting new members, be sure to work with your existing representatives.

Avon offers a lot of training, and you can provide further training. This is a relationship business. There are many ways to consistently create a community while training people through:
• social media
• newsletters
• mass text messages
• emails
• face-to-face meetings
• teleconferences
• handwritten notes
• breakfast, lunch or dinner meetings
• gift giving
• public and private acknowledgement of hard work

Read everything you can. Constantly read and educate yourself on the direct-selling industry.

Work with a mentor. Find a mentor, not a crutch. Create your own success and do not lean on someone else's accolades. Meet with your mentor and talk with other successful Avon sellers and leaders. Learn from their failures and successes.

Be a mentor. God wants me to lean on Him for all my needs. I acknowledge that He also puts certain people in my life for a reason. Always be open to learning and sharing.

Surround yourself with like-minded people. Winners breed winners. Work with people who want success at least as much as you do. Surround yourself with winners and people who want to put in the hard work to win.

Be consistent. Consistently commit to working hard for the success of your business. Let your actions speak volumes that you "believe."

Have fun. Work hard while having fun throughout the process. When people witness you and your team having fun, they want to learn more. Always remember, you are your own boss. You set the rules. Enjoy the journey toward realizing your dreams. Laugh!

I hope my story gives you the courage to step out in faith even when it does not make sense. Believe in yourself even when you want to give up. Most importantly, trust in the Lord at all times!

While building your business:
• Ignore naysayers.
• Trust in God.

- Continue prospecting for new representatives, and remember your existing team members.
- Strive to consistently motivate, encourage, and train your people, and yourself.
- Have patience, and avoid resting on your past successes.
- Press for more. Dream big!
- Use all resources available to connect with your people and other winners.

The activities you do each day move your dream toward becoming a reality. You do not need to possess an academic degree to be successful as an Independent Sales Representative and leader with Avon. You do need passion, drive, persistence, and the willingness to put the needs of others before your own. Recognize the good in all individuals you encounter, despite their differences. Most important, recognize the good in you!

S. DIANE MELTON, CAF, MBA, PhD

Avon® Executive Unit Leader
Author, National Recruiter,
Honor Society Member

404-721-2400
www.youravon.com/melton
www.startavon.com code: Melton

Diane joined Avon in April 2011 while teaching college-level business courses in higher education. She has over 200 people on her team, called *Through Grace and by Faith*. Diane has achieved President's Club each year since her first full year with Avon. Her team has generated over $1 million in team sales in the last 3.5 years.

Diane is trained in corporate sales and marketing. She has a bachelor's degree from the University of South Carolina, a master's in Business Administration from Hampton University, and PhD in Organization and Management with a specialization in Leadership from Capella University. She completed the Institute for Management and Leadership in Education at the Harvard University Graduate School of Education, where she served as one of the lead conveners.

Diane resides in the southeastern U.S., where she spends time with friends and family. She has 15 nieces and nephews—LaToya, Barry, Jr., Cierra, Jason, Jeremiah, Jordan, Kewanda, Courtney, Faran, Uriyah, Josiah, Amari, Grayson, Sky and Chase. She enjoys volunteering at senior communities, serving at church, staying fit, traveling, watching sports, and participating in outdoor activities such as hiking, biking and "glamping" (glamorous camping).

From Adversity to Prosperity

BY BRIAN AND JOANNA NEIDERHISER

I grew up as an only child in Pennsylvania. My childhood was difficult. I felt the stress of fighting parents who divorced, and my mother was ill with Lupus.

From the time I could walk, I tripped over my own feet. I had to wear Forrest Gump-like braces from my hips down. That was grueling to endure, as other kids were quite cruel.

To make ends meet, my mother worked odd jobs like cleaning houses and caring for elderly people. I always accompanied her. She looked out for others and made sure my needs were met. She taught me how to persevere and really stretch a dollar.

Storms Make Trees Take Deeper Roots

When I was 13 and making money babysitting, I started buying my own school clothes and shoes. I no longer had braces on my legs and made up for lost time by indulging in my deep love of cute shoes. I wanted to be a model.

After high school, I attended a two-year college. My father became very ill, and I took time off to care for him. During that time, I got married and had two beautiful children, Kyle and Colton. Although my marriage ended, we have remained active parents and friends.

I worked for a durable medical equipment company where I learned to meet deadlines and to set and accomplish goals. I discovered I liked being competitive and having a focused direction. Little did I know, those skills would prepare me for my future Avon® career.

A New Beginning

In the summer of 1997, a friend, Brian Neiderhiser, asked me to attend a banquet with him, and I gladly accepted. He was the one meant for me. We married in 2002. We were blessed with a son, Nathaniel.

> *"Trust in the Lord with all your heart*
> *and lean not on your own understanding; in all your ways*
> *submit to him, and he will make your paths straight."*
> **—Proverbs 3:5-6, The Bible**

Then, after 16 years at my job, I was laid off. No one can be prepared for the feeling of that devastation. However, just past the devastation, I found joy. During the first week, my kids were home with me for four days. I suddenly had a new freedom. Those moments with my boys were truly precious. We made cookies and hot chocolate, and built a huge snow fort! This is how I wanted, and needed, to spend my time.

To fill the gap in income not covered by my unemployment check, I found a part-time office job. My new boss did not allow me to call and check on my children after school, and that did not sit right with me. I asked my church for prayers concerning my job situation. The next week, a lady from my church asked if I would help her with her cleaning business. I said yes, quit my job, and never went back to an office job again.

I helped her during the day and was home for the kids in the afternoon. Although I was making good money, my unemployment payments would soon run out. I needed to find something else fast.

I attended a local fair with my family in August 2007 and was introduced to Avon. I did not dream big enough in the beginning and did not realize everything Avon had to offer. When I saw all the ways to make money with my new business, the sky became the limit.

Joining Avon helped me realize I did not like having a boss, being told what to do, nor sitting in an office. Things began to become clear personally and professionally. Even though our circumstances are not always ideal, they define us and mold us into the people we become. I could have been angry or upset about my circumstances; however, when given lemons, you must make lemonade.

> *"You must do the one thing you think you cannot do."*
> **—Eleanor Roosevelt, former First Lady of the United States**

I am not the same person I was when I joined Avon in 2007. It has changed me for the better. I have developed new skill sets, including public speaking—something I never envisioned for myself because I did not have the self-confidence. As I have set and reached goals, stepped out of my comfort zone repeatedly, and watched others succeed because of their hard work and my coaching, I have let go of the fear. Now I believe I can achieve anything I set my mind to.

In my early Avon days, my manager would ask me to share something about my business with a room full of my peers. The words stuck in my throat and I could not speak. She saw my potential and continued to encourage me. I loved to help, yet struggled with the confidence to speak in front of people. Thankfully, she did not give up and helped me overcome my fears. Today I finally believe in myself.

My husband, Brian, has been my biggest support. He believed in me and helped me overcome many personal fears. He saw me growing beyond what I thought myself capable of. He and our children have always played active roles in our Avon business. It is a T.E.A.M. effort. Together everyone achieves more.

A pivotal moment for me was when I was chosen to participate in Avon's National Leadership Council, along with nine other representatives from the United States. I could not believe it. That year, I shared my ideas with decision makers regarding how we conducted our entire program. I realized I had a voice and could make a difference.

Over time, I gained confidence and refined my public speaking. I had found my voice! I began holding regular team meetings and leading meetings for our area. In 2014, I was asked to be a guest speaker at Avon's National Conference. That was the beginning of something greater than I could ever imagine. I found me.

When you help others grow in areas where you are already successful, it feels even more rewarding. Your business begins to flourish. Do not stop growing and learning.

> *"If you can believe it, you can achieve it."*
> **—Walt Disney, American business magnate,**
> **filmmaker and philanthropist**

My biggest blessing from my business is the lifestyle it provides. When my stepfather was ill and placed on hospice care, I was able to have him in my home for three weeks. I love being my own boss and choosing my own schedule. I no longer miss any of my children's events and am free to join my husband for lunch.

My childhood dream was to be a model, yet modeling school was too expensive. Nevertheless, Avon has made my modeling dream come true! When I participated in the making of a training video in New York, I knew that God had placed me where I was supposed to be. I was featured in the *What's New* publication and got my fill of being a "model," just like I had always wanted.

Living the Good Life

When I joined Avon, I mistakenly thought leadership would take me away from my family, and so I focused only on selling for my first two years. I did not know that leadership and Avon incentives would provide many memory-making opportunities with our children. My income allows us to travel, attend sporting events, and do other fun things we might not have been able to do otherwise.

In 2013, Brian and I traveled out of the country for the first time, to beautiful Jamaica—courtesy of Avon. I also enjoyed my first trip to Las Vegas completely free, from Avon. On our Avon journey, we have made lifelong friends who have turned into partnerships and support systems.

I strongly encourage you to look at each incentive Avon offers and make a plan. Consistent behavior over time rewards greatly. You earn the prize and gain stability as your team grows.

Avon has allowed me to help others monetarily and to be a part of something greater. I get to volunteer at a senior center and also enjoy painting nails for ladies who have not had their nails done in twenty years. I have the freedom to help someone who does not drive by driving them to the store—because I can.

With hard work and dedication, and showing others how to duplicate the process, you can have anything you want—and so can they. Never give up, and always believe in yourself.

One Day at a Time

Starting anything new can be overwhelming. Surround yourself with like-minded people who support you. Write down your goals and focus on what works for you. This is *your* race, and how you run it depends on you!

Here are a few things that have helped me succeed:
- **Be your best customer.** Use Avon products so you have a personal testimony to share with others.
- **Brand yourself.** You are the Avon lady while running errands. Make it a habit to wear an Avon pin, carry an Avon bag, and always have samples. Talk about Avon to five people daily.
- **Manage your time.** Without a boss, it is up to you to determine what you need to accomplish each day, what hours to work, and what to schedule. Leave ample time for family.
- **Use your earnings chart.** Before submitting orders, make sure that you are not on the cusp of the next earning level.

When a Window Closes, a Door Opens

My decision to join leadership came during a *One Week to Unit Leader* class led by Teresa Ficara. She presented the Avon opportunity as a gift I could give. A light bulb came on. It had not occurred to me that I could change lives by offering the gift of Avon. Teresa said that just because people do not run around with a sign on their forehead saying that they need money, it does not mean that they don't.

I was then challenged to spend 25 hours with my manager, learning how to prospect and talk to strangers. She encouraged me to approach people. Although it was uncomfortable, I managed to make Unit Leader.

The very first person we approached that week actually joined my team and is still a Unit Leader today. My first check as a Leadership representative was $17.71. You have to start somewhere, and that was just the beginning. You find team members by consistently talking to new people every day.

Five Success Strategies

1. Value personal development. Participate on calls, attend meetings, and read inspirational books.

2. Dream. Create dream boards with your team. If you have a bad day, pull yours out and dream about where you are going, not where you are now.

3. Encourage your team members to work toward their goals. You cannot do the work for someone. Show her how, and then let her be independent.

4. Invest in your business. Leadership money is investment money, like a 401K. The more you put into your business, the more you get out of it.

5. Recognize team members. People love to be noticed and recognized for their efforts. Praise and reward your team for a job well done!

Working with someone from the beginning and watching her grow with you is the most rewarding gift of all for a leader.

Are You Doing All You Can?

We all experience challenges. I was struggling as an Advanced Unit Leader when I earned a business planning session with Avon's Evertrue Bell. It changed my vision and steered my success. We looked at where my business was and where it could be in four years. By working a little harder, my team and I achieved more. In 2011, I achieved Executive Unit Leader.

In 2013, I had a setback to my goal of becoming Senior Executive Unit Leader. I was on the verge of reaching my ultimate goal when one of my top leaders left Avon. I had to start over. It was disappointing, yet I did not give up. I moved on and found my next leader, who is motivated. You can overcome the obstacles. Do not quit.

Brian's Point of View

Life as an "Avon husband" is challenging and also rewarding! Many representatives complain that their spouses or partners do not support them. They may be equating paychecks with work hours—flawed thinking in a multi-level marketing business. In the beginning, the hours are long and hard and the pay is low. Over time, you will see the gradual shift to pay equaling the workload. Eventually you will get to a point—and a hefty six-figure income—where the pay far exceeds the work! Focus on that goal.

Advice to spouses or partners:
• Although you may work hard at your job and be tired when you come home, providing a little help goes a long way.

- If your spouse or partner loves the business, you should too. If it is important to him or her, it should be important to you. Make an effort to get involved.
- A business run with family help grows faster and is more profitable, benefiting everyone. I sacrifice time with Joanna while she is out working and helping her team. I also receive the reward of her business profitability. I have traveled to Jamaica, New York and Orlando, and have enjoyed many awesome Avon dinners. I love to see the excitement on Joanna's face when she earns something. Her smile is sometimes all it takes to know she is where she needs to be.
- Do your best to attend Avon events. It shows your support, and you see the business firsthand. Being involved has changed my perspective, and I have made lifelong friends along the way.

I recently attended my first conference where Joanna was a speaker. I was more nervous than she was, even though I saw the day coming a long time before she ever did. I see the passion she has and the stress she puts on herself, helping her team to become more successful. We have experienced firsthand the benefits of Avon with the life we have been able to create. Joanna is prepared to share that gift with *everyone* she meets.

To succeed there are no magic words or secrets. It starts with you. What are you willing to do today that others are not? Do something every day to grow your business. Be willing to practice until you can comfortably talk to anyone, any time. You can overcome the fear of prospecting. Start sharing Avon's life-changing gift with others today.

BRIAN AND JOANNA NEIDERHISER
Avon® Executive Unit Leader
Leadership council, mentor,
national recruiter
724-331-9533
jobu615@yahoo.com
www.youravon.com/jneiderhiser
www.facebook.com/joanna.neiderhiser

Brian and Joanna reside in Connellsville, Pennsylvania, and are the proud parents of three boys and a dog named Bella. Joanna started with Avon after she was laid off from the corporate world.

Joanna's team has received numerous awards for sales increases and recruiting excellence. Many members have earned the Spirit of Avon award. Joanna and Brian have held a spot in the top three in the Division each year since becoming Executive Unit Leader in C7 of 2012. Brian and Joanna's business generated over $700,000 at the close of 2013. They have earned Avon trips to amazing locations, including Jamaica and Las Vegas. Joanna has been featured in the *What's New* and *Avon Pathway* training videos, and has been a speaker at Avon's 2014 conference in Orlando, Florida.

Joanna's goal is to run a million dollar business and to show others how to do the same. Her mottos are:

- It's not what you *say,* it's what you *do.*
- It's not how you *start,* it's how you *finish.*
- It's not who you *are,* it's who you can *become.*
- It's not yet too late to *change.*
- Through Christ, all things *are* possible.

Rough Diamonds

Polish for Maximum Brilliance

BY BERTA BENCH

I was born in Mexico City in 1964. My parents were humble workers from rural Mexico, who moved to the city just prior to my birth. They both worked hard to make ends meet for their large family of nine children. When I was a teenager, my older sister immigrated to the United States. When I was in my twenties, I came to stay with her.

Our family values were strong. I thank my sister for helping me come to the United States, where I was able to work cleaning homes. When I returned to Mexico City in 1987 to visit my family, I met a young man who was serving an LDS mission in Mexico City. The next year we reconnected in Wisconsin and were married that fall.

We are grateful to be the parents of six children. Andrew is a professional hairstylist. Tisha is a registered nurse. Weston is serving an LDS mission in Ecuador. Ryan is a certified nursing assistant and will soon be reporting for a mission to Brazil. Iris is attending high school. Garett is in middle school. Family and church are our most prized blessings.

Starting Out in Sales

When I was 12 years old, one of my neighbors started selling Avon® products to my mother. I became her helper and she paid me twenty percent. With that money, I started buying my own personal items as well as helping my family financially. I did this throughout high school. Little did I know that this early contact with Avon would later turn into the grand business opportunity I now have.

But back in those days, I was mainly busy with school, family and friends. I stopped selling. It was not until after I was married and living in Utah that I found another representative who asked me to be her helper. My husband was in college and working part time, and I was able to help with our family income through Avon.

In the early 1990s I joined a multi-level marketing company. I have always enjoyed sales, but the concept of MLM was new to me. I learned about the power of duplication. I worked with my father, who is an inspiration to me. When he was training a group of people, he told them that this type of business is for people with long-term vision and are hard workers. Drawing on his agricultural roots, he narrated a story to convey the power of residual income. There is a fertile field full of rocks. If you personally clear the land of all the rocks for minimal pay, then you earn the right to coordinate the cultivation of the field with other workers. For your effort, you will continue to receive payments on whatever is grown in the field, every day for the rest of your life. You will still have to supervise the work, but you will not have to do all of the cultivating, planting and harvesting. This was an intriguing concept for me. Residual income was my goal.

I looked into many different companies with this sales model and tried several. Then in 2002, when I was looking for some Moisture Therapy® hand cream, I found a local representative and ordered some products from her. She asked me if I wanted to sign up with the company and said it only cost $10. My kids were young—6 months to 11 years old—and I was a stay-at-home mom. This was a perfect business that I could do from home, without leaving my kids. Later I found that this was also a business that my kids and husband could be actively involved in.

After signing up, I was going through my kit and came across information on the leadership program. I was speechless. I knew that the Avon products were good and that the prices were affordable; however, I did not know that they had implemented a multi-level marketing design. I did not start the leadership program right away, as I knew it would be a major time commitment. I waited almost a year before starting to build my business.

I began by delivering brochures door to door. With the help of my wonderful manager, Rory Clark, I became Unit Leader in one campaign. After four months at unit leader, I decided I wanted to take my business to a higher level. That is when the whole family got involved.

Growing the Business

My husband would drive the car, taking hundreds of brochures. I would supervise the "ground crew" consisting of Andrew, age 11, and Ryan, age 5, delivering brochures on one side of the street, and Tisha, age 10, and Weston, age 7, delivering on the other side of the street. I would take some side streets, and then we would all meet up with my husband at the end of the street. We did that every week for many campaigns.

I am not what you would call "technology savvy." Placing orders electronically was difficult for me, and my husband had to place the orders electronically for a whole year. Once, when my husband was away on a trip, I had to place the order by myself. I ended up sending it erroneously twice. When I got the order, I was so upset with myself that I decided I had to leave the Stone Age and become more comfortable with the Internet.

In four months, I became Executive Unit Leader (EUL). My manager, Diane White, was a great support. One of my first helpers was my daughter, Tisha, who sold Avon to her friends at school.

In 2004, we moved to Rockford, Illinois, for my husband's residency training. Unfortunately, my group in Utah started declining. It was heartbreaking and discouraging. I realized that they relied on me a lot, maybe too much. I loved to motivate my group. I loved to help them, encourage them and incentivize them; however, I had made them dependent on me in many ways.

As I launched a new group in Rockford, with support from my manager, Connie Cruz, I tried to focus more on one representative at a time. I would teach her everything I knew and show her how to be a leader. Sometimes I had to start from the ground up, even teaching others how to use the computer to send in orders. Imagine that—me as a computer teacher! I saw representatives grow in independence, gain new skills, and become confident leaders.

After three years, we returned to Utah, leaving a small, yet steady group in Rockford. I was able to keep my title, but there were times I was at risk of losing it. I basically had to start over with my group in Utah, which had dwindled. My motivation and vision had dwindled as well. I felt like I was just treading water, barely maintaining, and not growing for the next three years.

In 2010, I decided it was time for me to either progress to Senior Executive Unit Leader (SEUL) or leave the business. I had dropped to Advanced Unit Leader, performing as a Unit Leader. I was at a breaking point. I again talked to my family, seeking their support for me to do Avon full time. This would be a sacrifice for everybody. I would need to be gone a lot. Then again, since my kids were older, they would be able to help more with the responsibilities at home.

Success

I dedicated seventy to eighty hours a week for seven months, achieving EUL again. Then in campaign 3, 2011, I became SEUL. I knew that the Nesting Program was in the works and that this would help grow my business. I wanted reach SEUL before then, which I did.

After much sacrifice, patience and dedication, and with support and inspiration from my managers, Sara Wilson and Jamie Loveland, I reached my goal.

The reward for this accomplishment was a cruise to Alaska. My husband came with me on this, his first cruise. He has always been supportive of my Avon activities, and this cruise seemed to peak his interest. He has never been rewarded a cruise by his employer! I made him learn to shout, "I love Avon!" which I often do. Now he does as well.

Joys of Leadership

I love seeing the people in my group progress in so many ways. I see sales representatives gain confidence as they talk with others. Some, like me, have started using the computer for the first time in their lives. Some have been inspired to start school to learn English so that they can have more sales opportunities. Some have learned to drive in order to deliver products to their clients. All have become better business women, growing in confidence and ability. They are becoming leaders for their own groups, inspiring and encouraging others.

I have made wonderful friendships, not just business associates. I have been inspired by other leaders' successes. I love to meet wonderful people at the Avon Summits, trips and conventions.

"Rough diamonds may sometimes be mistaken for worthless pebbles."
—Sir Thomas Browne, English author

My Rough Diamonds

When I meet new contacts, I see them as my rough diamonds. Everyone has potential to succeed in this business. First we become real friends. I am interested in them, their lives and their struggles. I become invested in their personal success. I have seen what extra income, earned with their new economic abilities, can do for them and their families. With patience and effort, they become great leaders with professional skills. Let me tell you how I found some of my rough diamonds.

- **Handing out brochures.** The first leader I found when I returned to Utah was Leonor. I found her when I was handing out brochures. She was expecting her third child. She was very shy, did not work outside her home, did not drive or speak English. She did not use the Internet. After ordering $30 of products, I asked her if she would like to be my helper. She did not say no, so I left her thirty brochures to hand out. I later found out that she had previously been a helper to someone who would sell her the brochures for $1. She thought she now owed me money for the brochures I had just given her, and she was too shy to say anything. She was a helper for a couple of campaigns. Then when I saw her sales, I told her that I was going to sign her up for leadership. She was too shy to say no. I helped her learn to recruit. Through Avon, she now speaks English, she has started driving, and she uses the Internet and social media much better than I do. She approaches people, trains her group, and is becoming a great leader.

- **Doing facials.** My second diamond, Aiko, already had great leadership skills. I had to find the right opportunity to introduce her to Avon and asked if I could do a facial for her and her friends. I was learning to do facials. This was a good way to get some practice. Her daughter and her sisters loved the products. This allowed us to talk about the business. I asked them if they wanted to sign up with Avon, which would allow them to get the products at a discount. I told them I was looking for leaders, and I would help them to grow their business. Aiko jumped at the opportunity, as she is a very business-oriented leader.

- **Extending the opportunity to all.** The third leader, Silvina, had been a helper to another representative for many years. Unfortunately, this representative never discussed leadership nor gave her the opportunity to sign up directly with Avon. Silvina was an acquaintance of my sister, who told her that I was in leadership in Avon and that she should sign up with me. Silvina is now a wonderful leader and the number one seller in my group. She is a makeup expert who knows how to keep her clients satisfied. She has become expert in training her downline as well.

The Avon opportunity has opened the door for me to develop as a person. My communication skills have improved. My confidence in myself and in others has increased. I can see potential in people who may not see it in themselves.

My success comes from sharing a vision of success. My young son, after attending a recruiting meeting with me, said, "Mom, you were talking so much!" He didn't think that talking was really "work." I told him, "I get paid for talking." But what I really do is motivate others to rise to their true potential, to help themselves and their families increase their earnings.

My greatest happiness is seeing the people in my group grow. My personal growth is just icing on the cake.

I use my earnings to help my family and others financially. Unfortunately, there has been tragedy among people in my organization as well. There have been kidney transplants, cancer diagnoses, and untimely accidents taking the lives of family members. Avon has been an anchor, both emotionally and financially, for many of us.

Success will come to you if you find your true motivation. With my business, I have chosen to polish rough diamonds. In doing so, I have also been polished myself. Learn from your downline. Just like you, they also will have successes and failures. They are a treasure trove of collective experience. Just because you are their leader, does not mean that you will suddenly have all of the answers to all of their problems. Sometimes, all they need to overcome their challenges is support and recognition for their efforts. Set goals for them, then give them the encouragement and confidence that they may not yet have. Their success will be your success.

BERTA BENCH

Avon® Senior Executive Unit Leader
I love Avon!

801-687-2044
avonbench@gmail.com
www.youravon.com/bbench

As a mother of six, Berta Bench has dedicated thousands of hours to teaching her children principles which will give them success in life. She often refers to her children as her jewels. She feels happiest when she is surrounded by her large extended family, often celebrating birthdays and special occasions with them. Her title "Tia Berta" is one that she wears with pride. She is a brand new grandmother, spoiling her granddaughter with Tiny Tillia®, Avon's brand of infant products.

Berta's love of others extends to her Avon business. She shares the joy that she has found in Avon with everyone she can. Her cell phone has become her constant companion as she communicates with her group of representatives. She loves recruiting, which gives her the opportunity to travel to many different states.

Berta celebrates the accomplishments of her downline even more than her own. She can often be found giving out a basket of Avon products to someone who has just reached her goal in sales or leadership. Berta honors those who have helped her succeed.

The Little Chinese Girl
with a Big Dream

BY FEANNY XU

On August 13, 1989, I said goodbye to my parents, sister and friends at the Shanghai Airport and took my first international flight to Toronto, Canada—the country I am now proud to call home. During the long flight, I thought about my life so far.

I was born in a small city about three hours by train from Shanghai. I was raised by my paternal grandparents, an aunt and a nanny—who all treated me as their little princess. My mother, a nurse, wanted to become a surgeon and went back to university a few weeks after I was born. My father lived in another city until he retired. When I was 11, my mother finished her internship and decided it was time for me and my four-year-old sister, who was living with my maternal grandparents, to move to Shanghai.

I soon realized that my life as a princess had ended. I had to learn how to buy groceries, look after my sister, and manage all the household chores. At age 14, I had to do everything on my own, with some help from a neighbor, for a whole year while my mother treated patients in another county.

Sometimes, when I felt sad, I would sit under the stairs and let my imagination soar. I dreamed of living abroad, traveling, and exploring the world. When I was sent to the countryside to be re-educated during the Chinese Cultural Revolution, only my dreams made me happy.

> *"You can have anything you want—if you want it badly enough. You can be anything you want to be, do anything you set out to accomplish if you hold to that desire with singleness of purpose."*
> **—Abraham Lincoln, former United States president**

When the 747 landed in Toronto, I got off the plane with two suitcases, a few U.S. dollars in my pocket, and my dreams. Wow! I was finally living abroad and starting my new life. I told myself that I would never go back to China. I would pursue my dreams in Canada.

The First Few Years in Canada

My life in Toronto was not as easy as I had expected. It was difficult to find work as a newcomer with extremely limited English. The owner of a dry cleaner took pity on me and offered me a job to steam and press 600 men's shirts a day. After eight months, I decided I had had enough. There was no opportunity for me to learn English there, and the heat was making me sick.

I understood that I had to be able to speak English fluently in order to find a better job. I went to an agency for nannies and quickly landed a job as a live-in caregiver for a Canadian family. During my work there, they helped me speak English properly, and I took courses in the evenings. After a year, I passed the English examination and began a full-time business course.

I left the Canadian family and rented my own apartment on the third floor of an old house. Every time it rained, I had to fix the roof myself, as my landlord was elderly and unable to do it. After my studies, I was assigned a co-op job at a government office and then found a regular office job. Every day, I traveled from office to office to conduct my work. I enjoyed the work outside. It kept my dreams of traveling around the world alive, and I continued to believe it would happen.

My Miracle Son—My Inspiration

"Life's challenges are not supposed to paralyze you, they're supposed to help you discover who you are."
—Bernice Johnson Reagon, American singer, composer, scholar and social activist

In March 1993, I met my husband, Jim, a native Canadian. Five years later, we found out we were going to have a baby. I was thrilled because I had thought it was too late for me. My son, Daniel, was born at 4 lbs. and 11 oz. in July 1998 by emergency C-section. I was worried that he did not cry when he entered the world. He was beautiful and I wanted to hold him; however, he had to be in an incubator hooked up with all kinds of tubes for the next three weeks. I visited him twice a day until he was able to go home.

A few months later, we noticed Daniel was not developing as a normal baby. He was very calm and slept with his hands in the air and feet straight up. He was not rolling over and had difficulty swallowing and eating. A CT scan revealed that Daniel had cerebral palsy— quadriplegia. Jim and I were shocked.

Our Financial Situation

My husband had difficulty accepting Daniel's disability. He knew our financial situation would make it difficult to raise a disabled child. I had no time to grieve the loss of experiencing a normal baby. Libraries were my resource to find out everything I could to help my son become the best he could be.

Daniel started intensive occupational and physiotherapies, and then speech and music therapies when he was ten months old. We had to pay for everything ourselves. Health insurance did not cover all the expenses and we did not have additional coverage for therapies. At age three, Daniel was diagnosed with autism and later with developmental disability.

After remortgaging our house twice, I realized I could not continue working at my husband's business. I had to find a way to make money quickly. Finding a regular job and working nine to five was not an option; Daniel's many needs had to be met and he had various appointments every week.

My Reason to Start Selling Avon

When Daniel was two, his babysitter brought an Avon brochure to our home. After Daniel went to sleep, I looked through the book and noticed the Anew® skin care products cost much less than the Lancôme® I had been using. I ordered Anew to give it a try, fell in love with it, and started using the whole regimen. My friends noticed the change in my skin and asked what I was using. They started to order through my Avon lady, and I soon became her helper.

In spring 2004, a friend suggested that I should be her Avon lady. She would buy directly from me, and I could make a little money to pay for part of Daniel's therapies. I laughed and said that I did not know how to sell Avon and had never sold anything in my life. She said it would only cost $20 (now $10) to join Avon. "If you don't like it, you can just walk away, but if you don't try, you will never know," she said. True, I had nothing to lose.

I started selling Avon on April 21, 2004. That evening, I watched the Rich and Famous DVD that was in the Avon bag. When I finished at 3:00 a.m., I told myself that if these Avon ladies—especially Lisa Wilber—can do it, so can I. A week later, with only 10 brochures, I placed my first order of almost $400. I ordered 100 brochures to start my second campaign. I put Daniel in a special stroller and walked around the neighborhood delivering brochures to every door, every store, and everywhere I could.

At the first sales meeting I attended, I met Donna who was selling over $130,000 a year and ranked #1 in personal sales in the Division. I asked what her secret was. Donna attributed her success to consistency and brochures—she ordered 1,500 brochures each campaign. Wow, she was receiving awards, bonuses, trophies and free trips! I told myself I would be there soon.

I had increased my sales rapidly and achieved President's Club in six months and sold over $30,000 in my first year with Avon. I achieved the David H. McConnell level, which required $60,000 sales, and was happy to receive the 50 percent discount for beauty products in my third year with Avon.

Leadership Was Meant for Me

Avon leadership selected me while I was waiting for Daniel to finish a music therapy session. I gave a brochure to another mother waiting for her son. The lady said she wanted to sell Avon and did not know how to get started. She was my first team member.

I did not realize I had to continue recruiting or that leadership had a time frame for achieving each level. I was scared to give brochures directly to strangers. My brochures went out with me and often returned with me. I knew I had to make my Avon business work, as I could not fit into a regular job and needed to support my family. I decided my brochures would talk to people for me. It worked! A second person joined and my team grew.

In July 2006, I went on my first fully paid leadership retreat trip to Scottsdale, Arizona, and met many successful Avon leaders from across Canada. I met Darline and was inspired by her positive attitude and accomplishments. She was the first Senior Executive Unit Leader (SEUL) in Canada and a President's Club Council member. Despite undergoing a heart operation, she continued her Avon business with her husband's help. On the last day of the trip, I named my team the Happy Kokopelli Group after I won a sterling silver necklace of Kokopelli. After that trip, I was sure I would be on every paid trip with Avon Canada. My dream to travel the world was going to come true!

Keep Going and Climbing

"Resolve says, 'I will.' The man says, 'I will climb this mountain. They told me it is too high, too far, too steep, too rocky, and too difficult. But it's my mountain. I will climb it. You will soon see me waving from the top or dead on the side from trying.'"
—Jim Rohn, American entrepreneur,
author and motivational speaker

I met Lisa Wilber in Toronto in September 2009. I remember asking what she would do if people decided to stop selling. She smiled and told me to shout out, "Next!" What a great word to keep in mind.

The road was not a straight highway. In the fall of 2009, when I was almost reaching the top pay level in leadership, I lost an Executive Unit Leader, two Advanced Unit Leaders, and two Unit Leaders simultaneously for different reasons. It hit my Avon business very hard. With no time to be discouraged, I set my mind to rebuilding. My leader, Jessica Yee, stood by me, and we worked to rebuild our group.

After years of work, many wonderful people have joined our group. I finally achieved SEUL in May 2013! Our Happy Kokopelli Group has been ranking #4 in Avon Canada and has been selling over $1,000,000 annually for the past several years.

Words of Wisdom

Set your ultimate goal. Expect the most and you will have the most. I started my Avon business with the goal that my business would bring me the income I needed to support my son's special needs even when I was not around. You must see the view from the top before you can get there.

See things as they will be. Everyone's results are different. We all come from different backgrounds, have different reasons and different talents. Help people find what they love to do and what their talents are. Encourage them to use their specialties to build their business the way they want.

Success comes from within you. Discover why you want to build your business. Your reason and desire to reach your goal is going to help you get where you want to be. I knew I had to make my Avon business work for me, and that was my only choice. I had to focus on my ultimate goal and get there. Nothing was going to stop me.

Love What You Do and Do What You Love

"Choose a job you love, and
you will never have to work a day in your life."
—Confucius, Chinese teacher, editor, politician and philosopher

In 2014, we celebrated my 25th year of living in Canada, my son Daniel's 16th birthday, and my 10th Avon anniversary. Time flies! With the help of his support worker, Cecilia, Daniel learned to roll over, sit up, crawl, walk using a walking ladder, use a utensil and much more. My Avon income helps me to pay for the help I need for Daniel, for his wheelchair lift van, and for modifying our home to accommodate his special needs.

I am thankful to my son. Because of Daniel, I have found the work I love! I love to celebrate each and every accomplishment of my team members. I love to see my girls become the confident and successful individuals they were meant to be. I love the many Avon friends I have made over the years and who will be with me for a lifetime. I love to help people find out who they really are and work toward their goal. I love to be able to travel the world. Most of all, I love to see who I have become and love my Avon business—thanks to Daniel, who continues to inspire me to do even better.

My Biggest Dream

In May 2014, I landed in Toronto. This time I was not coming from China, but from Barcelona after a six-day trip, fully paid by Avon Canada. Since my first Avon trip to Arizona, Avon Canada has awarded me with 11 fully paid trips including Montego Bay, New York, Cancun, Punta Cana, Barbados, Paris, Prague, and my most recent trip to Barcelona. Traveling around the world—a little Chinese girl's big dream comes true!

My biggest dream now is to be able to continue supporting my son and help other children like him to develop to the best of their ability. Our Happy Kokopelli Group hopes to build a facility for helping special needs children.

Everyone has a dream. Believe that your dreams will come true if you set your mind to it. Sometimes, dreams get bigger and bigger after you achieve the first one. This happened to me.

Dreams Do Come True

"All our dreams can come true,
if we have the courage to pursue them."
—Walt Disney, American business magnate

I am thankful to Avon for the wonderful opportunity to make my dreams come true. Thanks to Cecilia and my husband, Jim, for believing in me even before I started selling Avon. Thanks to my amazing manager, Claudia, who believes in me and supports my team and me. Thanks to my awesome friends, to my fantastic team members, and to my loyal customers who have been there for me each and every step of the way.

Avon truly changes women's lives in many ways. I have become the confident person I was meant to be. I found what I love to do and discovered my love of helping others.

Wow, can you imagine an ESL student from China became a million dollar Avon business owner in Canada? Do you have a dream? Believe it will come true. Take action now and do not give up on your dream. Soon, you will be living in your dream, too!

FEANNY XU

Avon® Senior Executive Unit Leader
Founder of the Happy Kokopelli Group
416-222-9982
800-280-6823 (toll free for Canada)
feanny.avon@yahoo.ca
www.feannyxu.com
www.interavon.ca/feanny.xu

Feanny Xu dreamed of living abroad and traveling the world as a young child in China. Her dream came true when she arrived in Toronto as an ESL student in August of 1989 to pursue her dreams.

In April 2004, Feanny started her Avon business to support her son, Daniel, who was born with cerebral palsy and was later diagnosed with autism and developmental disability. Her Avon earnings pay for all of his personal care, therapies, wheelchair lift van and home modifications.

Feanny was a guest speaker at the Avon Canada National Conference in August 2008. Her Happy Kokopelli Group has been ranking #4 in Avon Canada. She has earned 12 fully paid trips including Paris, Prague and Barcelona. Her dream to travel around the world came true with Avon. Feanny's passion for helping others and appreciation for individuality has made her leadership style unique. She is determined to be a top earner with Avon so that she will be able to build a facility for disabled children and to assist them to be their best.

Blend Life with Success

BY LINDA MONTAVON

I had a normal childhood until, at the age of 14, I became so ill the doctors said I had about three days to live. I was 5' 7" and only weighed 58 pounds. Thankfully, the doctors were wrong. Still, the road to recovery was slow. I had become so weak I had to learn to eat and walk again, and I missed almost an entire semester of school. I learned early that miracles happen and to count every day as a blessing.

In high school, my motto was *work hard for what you want*. I studied a lot and graduated as salutatorian, ranking second out of 572 classmates. Although people labeled me as smart and likely to succeed, many in my graduating class were equally smart, if not smarter, more gifted and talented, and more well rounded than I was. I just worked extra hard.

After college, I got married and wanted nothing more in the world than to be a mom. In 1981 I gave birth to our son, Steven. Two years later our daughter, Erin, was born. I could not love two human beings more. I wanted to be "best mom" and a role model they would always respect. It is challenging to blend motherhood with a career, yet I thought I could pull it off.

After my husband and I moved our family from Missouri to Virginia, I landed a position with the Department of the Army. I had a great family and a great job. What could be better? Unfortunately, along with my secure, fabulous job came sacrifice. Sometimes I was assigned projects that turned my day job into a day and night job, or even a day, night and weekend job.

I was the go-to person to get things accomplished, held a top secret clearance, assisted administratively during Desert Storm, got promotions, and had an impressive resume. However, something was completely wrong. I wanted nothing more than to be an awesome and extraordinary wife and mom; yet between the commute and the hours, I was far from extraordinary. I merely survived. Then, after ten years of marriage, my husband and I divorced. I felt like a total failure.

When I met Richard, my current husband, I felt like I was given a second chance. Hoping to learn from past mistakes, I was determined to find balance. My family deserved it and I was on a mission to find a way to put family first while generating an adequate income.

I took a leave of absence from the government and had my third child, Charles (CJ). I pursued different business opportunities and nothing worked out. Keeping family the priority while still having a career proved to be much more challenging than I had expected.

I opened a daycare believing it would be the ideal solution. I loved children and could be there with mine. Unfortunately, my husband worked nights and slept during the day. It was unfair to the children to have to be quiet, and my husband needed his rest. Once again, something had to change.

While I was on a quest to find the ideal job, I began experiencing terrible breakouts on my skin. Although I spent ridiculous amounts of money in search of a solution, nothing worked. Then I ordered an Avon® cream and could not believe the results. It made my skin look great, and I instantly fell in love with Avon products.

The Perfect Solution

One day, my husband asked me if I ever considered becoming an Avon representative. I wanted nothing to do with selling anything—I was shy, reserved around strangers and very private. I quickly dismissed his suggestion. However, because I liked so many of the Avon products, I joined the company in November 1997 to get discounts, and this launched my Avon career.

Initially, I loved the flexibility. I could adjust the business to fit my needs. I ran my daycare during the day and delivered orders at night and on weekends. Then a flyer came in my order, with an incentive for sharing the Avon opportunity with others. I was excited because I thought Avon was the perfect fit for everyone. The products were awesome, the prices were incredible, and you had so many product choices—all backed with a 100 percent satisfaction guarantee. The way I saw it, everyone on the planet should be a representative, as it was the best deal in town. Two campaigns later, I started sharing the Avon opportunity with others and soon made it my career.

Because I was shy, I became the queen of *indirectly* building my business. I would leave brochures anywhere I could. I wore Avon clothing and jewelry, and always had a brochure sticking out of my purse. If there was a way to promote Avon without opening my mouth and sharing, I was doing it.

All that changed when my district sales manager offered an incentive. You could earn a free gift card to a restaurant if you did everything indicated on an Avon bingo card. I wanted it to reward my family. To earn it, I would have to knock on doors as well as talk and offer Avon to everyone I came in contact with. To say I was terrified is an understatement. My husband and my youngest son supported me by driving alongside me as I walked door to door. Most people were not home, but those who were at home were very nice and friendly. Once I stepped outside my comfort zone, I realized I had nothing to fear. It was actually fun sharing Avon.

> *"Move out of your comfort zone. You can only grow*
> *if you are willing to feel awkward and uncomfortable*
> *when you try something new."*
> **—Brian Tracey, Canadian entrepreneur,**
> **public speaker, author and trainer**

Misfortune Arrives

Then life became a blur. My husband, Richard, suffered knee, shoulder, and back injuries and underwent 9 surgeries in the first 12 years I was with Avon. He had excruciating pain and slow recovery periods in addition to developing type 2 diabetes and asthma.

Richard was out of work for extended periods of time, cutting his pay drastically. We were fortunate to have Avon, which allowed me to care for my loved ones and continue to earn much needed money.

Another big scare came in 2010 when CJ suffered a concussion and fractured his back while wrestling. Thankfully, he recovered.

During this time period, not only did my business continue, it grew. I sometimes worked unusual hours and at strange locations like the hospital waiting area. With the flexibility Avon offers, I was able to make Avon work for us. We needed the money to offset medical bills and keep family finances in order. Was it easy? No. However, Avon did allow me to blend life with success. I could be there for my family, attend activities, volunteer and earn money.

Strategies for Success

Have a plan, show up for work, share Avon, and you can build a successful business.

- **Train and work with leaders who want to work.** While building my team, I made the mistake of doing most of the work and was not duplicable. As a result, when I stopped doing all the work for others, I lost most of my leaders and had to start over. I learned the hard way to attract true leaders and not people who only show up to collect the reward.
- **Do not compare yourself to others.** I watched a top representative in my district approach strangers and talk to them as they got in or out of their cars. I was stunned and almost left Avon because I thought I would have to do that too. Instead, I figured out what I was good at and made Avon work for me.
- **Get contact information.** Do not just wait for people to call and express interest. When offering Avon, get their contact information so you can follow up.
- **Clarify your *why*.** Understand why you started Avon. Make a vision board and place it where you will always see it. Visualize your dreams every day so that working your business is fun and moves you closer to what you want. No dream or goal is too big or too small.
- **Remember your accomplishments.** Helping and empowering others to fulfill dreams is extremely rewarding. People have told me their children will have Christmas, food or shoes because of

their Avon business. What an impact this made on me. Of course the trips, cash and various incentive rewards are also gratifying.

- **Keep your business simple.** Share the opportunity to join your team with everyone you talk to and include a recruiting flyer in every brochure. If you only look for customers, that is all you will find. If you share the Avon opportunity first, you will build both your team and sales. Do this consistently, and show your leaders how to do the same. Business will boom.

- **Develop your skills.** If you need more customers, focus on how to get them. It may take trial and error until you find what works for you. For instance, when I used customer appreciation events to find recruits, I told people we were having a customer appreciation day and encouraged them to register for our drawing to win $50 in free products. No one wanted to register. Then I tried inviting people to sign up. That did not work either because it sounded like a commitment. When I simply offered the opportunity to enter the drawing, people said yes. I found words that worked for me.

- **Partner with other successful representatives.** Partnering is a great way to enhance everyone's skills, improve your business and develop long-term friendships.

- **Ask for help and brainstorm with others.** Let everyone know your current goal and ask for help. People like to help. They can help you find events, fundraisers, people who need more money or people looking for something to do. They can help you think of places to go and people who would be interested in the Avon brochure or opportunity. They can help you get business and give you referrals.

- **Make Avon part of your day.** Everywhere you go, connect with people. Have conversations and extend your services. I start by saying hello with a smile. Chitchat begins, and before you know it I can connect a topic to Avon. For instance, Maxine, a housekeeper, mentioned that she wanted money to visit her family. I could then easily offer Avon as a means to earn money. She joined because Avon was a good fit and met her needs.

- **Set goals.** Be clear on your annual income goal, know your long-term plan for advancement, and review goals regularly to make sure you are on target. Break your goals down, and decide what you want to earn each campaign. Determine how many customers you need to serve and how many business partners you need to get started in order to earn that amount. Be consistent, have a plan and then work the plan.
- **Give back to the community.** Ask groups and organizations if they need to raise money. You can help organizations earn money through quality products without inflated prices, and your business gets great exposure.
- **Utilize social media.** While this may take time, it is another way of gaining sales and recruits.
- **Never prejudge.** It is not up to you to determine if Avon is right for someone or not. Let people choose what is right for them—whether it is being a representative, a helper, a customer, or to give you referrals. It is actually the thoughtful thing to do when you offer and let people choose whether they are interested or not, and not make the decision for them.
- **Plan your calendar.** Work the hours you have dedicated to your business and schedule activities that generate income. Customize this to fit your personality. It may be going door-to-door, business-to-business, a community yard sale, or setting up a table at your local bank, favorite restaurant, or grocery store. Just be sure there is business on your books.

Keep Going When Things Get Tough

Let's face it; not every day is going to be sunshine and roses. Once, I had seven appointments scheduled. I left my house at 7:30 a.m. and got home at 8:30 p.m., and every appointment was a cancelation or a no-show. I came home exhausted and with nothing to show for my day's efforts. That was a terrible day, yet I felt grateful knowing not every day was like that.

Commit to the long haul. One of my most advanced leaders had the craziest beginning with leadership. We drove forty minutes to meet with someone who did not show up. Then, she thought she locked her keys in her car, and we called a tow truck. When it arrived an hour later, there were no keys inside the car. We spent the next hour looking for her keys. Thank goodness someone eventually turned them in. That was not a great way to start her leadership career; however, she persevered because she needed to pay her taxes and wanted to make Unit Leader in one campaign. It took her two campaigns to earn the money she needed. She has since become a top leader and a top seller.

Keep Learning, Keep Growing

Coach and role play with your team members; do not tell them what to do. If you help them create their own plan, they are more committed to it. In the past, when team members expressed challenges, I would immediately share my strategies. However, that was not effective because it was not their plan. Now when they call, I ask questions and ask what they have already tried. Then I ask them what they think they can do or change to overcome their challenge. This makes it their plan.

With practice, everything in your business becomes easier. Even if there are tasks you do not enjoy, do them anyway. The more you do something, the more comfortable it becomes.

Know how you spend your earnings. One representative loved Disney World®, and her Avon earnings allowed her to take her kids there several times in one year. Some representatives have paid cash for a car, traveled, or saved for a home. My Avon income paid unexpected hospital bills and bought Christmas presents. It paid for braces, unexpected house and car expenses, vacations and college tuition. Knowing the money you earned has made a difference will keep you going and growing, and may help others visualize Avon being right for them too.

Be proud of your journey whether you make it to your goal quickly or slowly. Remember, both the tortoise and the hare can cross the finish line.

> *"The future belongs to those who believe*
> *in the beauty of their dreams."*
> **—Eleanor Roosevelt, former First Lady of the United States**

Persevere and always know in your heart that you can be successful. And remember to have fun while building your business, enjoying both life and Avon. Life is a blessing, so make every moment count.

LINDA MONTAVON

Avon® Executive Unit Leader
866-avonyes (866-286-6937)
www.youravon.com/yes
www.facebook.com/lindamontavonavon
www.facebook.com/groups/
montavonclimbers
www.youtube.com/user/lindamontavon

Linda left the traditional workforce seeking a way to keep family first while still having a viable means of earning money. Little did she know the company she joined to get a discount on her products would be the answer. Linda had no sales experience and was very shy, yet she was still able to excel with Avon. Linda has reached an impressive status with her sales, and by sharing her love of Avon with others, she holds an elite status with team building and team sales. Although she has earned many trips and trophies, she remains most proud of earning the "prestigious" Spirit of Avon award twice. This is an award given because of an attitude of giving, sharing and selflessness, and having a spirit that stands out above the rest. Linda has been a featured speaker and presenter at numerous events and venues, is a Certified Beauty Advisor and Anew Skincare Specialist, and is DSWA Elite Leadership certified.

When she is not working, Linda enjoys socializing with family and friends, reading, and spending time with her husband, three children and all her adorable grandbabies.

Believe and Achieve

BY HEATHER MURRAY

You will achieve when you believe. The first step in any challenge you face is believing that you can conquer and overcome it.

> *"Whatever it is you may be going through,*
> *I know He's not gonna let it get the best of you."*
> —**Mandisa, American Christian recording artist**

Many of us wallow in what could have been, what was, or what should be. I encourage you to focus on the present and the future. You cannot change your past. You *can*, however, shape your future. Do you want more of what you have or do you want a life you deserve and can attain? Have you explored the greatness within you?

It Starts with Belief

I was born and raised in Philadelphia. After I graduated college, I moved to Fort Pierce, Florida, to be an elementary school teacher. I believed I could change the lives of young children in an impoverished area. During that time, I joined Avon® to get a discount on my orders. Becoming an Avon lady was a pivotal time in my life.

A few years later, my husband, Sean, and I were blessed with our first child. I wanted to be a stay-at-home mom, yet still needed to earn money. We believed that Avon could replace my teaching income and made a plan to achieve it.

The turning point for my Avon career came the moment I became a mother. My priorities and opportunities changed and so did my focus. Instead of continuing to sell to a handful of customers in the neighborhood and at work, I needed to restructure my business to generate more income. I needed to step out of my comfort zone and talk to people.

When our baby was one year old, we justified my stay-at-home role knowing that the company I represented could provide a discount on my personal products, a commission on products sold, and a residual income based on what my leadership team sales were each cycle. We were making money!

Work Hard, Play Hard

Customers give you the "right now" money. When you balance that with your downline team, you get residual income.

While building my team, I earned many district and national incentives, including four televisions and plenty of trips. I went to the Bahamas, Las Vegas, Orlando and Miami. We earned a free Keurig® coffee maker, free coffee for an entire year, and an Avon popcorn machine. The formula for earning Avon incentives is to read about the incentive offered, make a clear plan to accomplish the goals, and take action.

My business ensures our family bills are paid and provides for extras. Big or small, the dream is achievable. I have used my earnings to purchase the car of my dreams—a Ford Mustang®. It felt incredible to pay cash for it! What do you want in your driveway? Work for it, and you can exceed your expectations to have the car of your dreams.

When Avon offered an incentive for a free cruise to the Bahamas, it signified a pivotal point in my journey. First of all, it introduced me to the extraordinary rewards Avon offers to representatives. It also taught me how to be proactive and set goals to earn the incentive. Along the way, I made extra money and partnered with team members to attain their dreams. We worked together to schedule our time effectively, and I did earn that free trip.

Avon trips are top notch. The company pays for your transportation, accommodations, meals, and goodie bags filled with newly launched Avon products. Meeting and sharing perspectives with top-level representatives from around the country is always the highlight.

After giving birth to our second daughter, I left for that all-expenses-paid cruise. It was beautiful, rejuvenating, exciting, and taught me that I wanted to keep working for this fantastic company and climb to the top of the pay plan. You can optimize time in your schedule to accomplish the goals you set and establish a legacy for your family.

My Avon business has rewarded me with much more than money, prizes and awards. It has molded me into a better public speaker and role model. I was already comfortable speaking in public, having taught school for years; however, I no longer teach young children to read books. I am now a teacher, partner, and friend to men and women on their way to better lives.

It starts with belief. Redesign your atmosphere by designating an area of your home to your Avon business. Engage in positive thoughts and actions by connecting with local representatives and other role models to expand your horizons. Believe and achieve!

Trials and Tribulations

"Trust the Lord with all your heart,
and lean not on your own understanding."
—Proverbs 3:5, The Bible

One day, my best friend died suddenly, at a young age, of undetermined natural causes. The next day, I took a pregnancy test, and it was positive. Going through those two experiences at the same time was difficult. Not to mention, I was "this close" to the next leadership level. My business did not progress as planned that year and we needed to reevaluate some aspects of it. There were bumps in the road, yet we did not detour or turn back.

Continue to push forward and be a positive influence on those around you. Enjoy today and dream of tomorrow. Introduce a plan to make the dream a reality. Do not let the troubles of life sway or stop you. Learn the lesson and pass along the knowledge.

My three beautiful daughters are my blessings and my legacy. I believe in passing along to them my values and traditions—as well as the income this company has provided.

Strategies from the Front Lines

"You get what you put in, and people get what they deserve."
—Kid Rock, American singer and multi-instrumentalist

The above lyrics are from a song that touches me on many levels. The bottom line is that you can get what you deserve after you first put in the work to get there. The beauty of Avon is that you can work one hour a week or eighty hours a week, as long as you realize you will not get eighty hours worth of pay for one hour of work.

I encourage you to schedule time in your calendar for when you will actively talk to people about Avon. In addition to emails, texts and social media, focus on face-to-face interaction with family, friends, and people you chat with while standing in line at the store. Set specific, measurable goals for how much money you want to earn this week. What steps will you implement to make it happen?

- Write down the steps on paper.
- Put yellow sticky notes on your bathroom mirror to remind you of your goals.
- Make tasks simple.
- Commit to the task. Keep brochures, samples and business cards in your car.
- Smile when you talk to potential customers and maintain a cheerful and uplifting attitude.

Thirty-Second Elevator Speech

When you take an elevator, do you stand there quietly, become distracted by your cell phone, or strike up a conversation with the person standing next to you? Develop a quick and to-the-point statement to brand you and the company you represent. Here are examples of my thirty-second "commercials," which I say with a smile and revise depending on my audience.

At the pediatrician's office:
Hello, my name is Heather and I help stay-at-home moms like you

start their own home-based business to be able to pay for daily needs and provide for their children's future.

To a bank teller:
Hello, my name is Heather and I help professional men and women like you provide additional income to be able to go on tropical vacations and rejuvenate at the best hotels.

If you are a sales representative, you can adjust the script to focus on the daily needs and outstanding values you offer through the Avon brochure or your online personal website:
Hello, my name is Heather and I provide affordable products and reliable service to busy men and women in the neighborhood. I also have an online website for quick and easy shopping.

Then, *listen* to people's responses. Incorporate why they might want to join your team. Focus on *them*. Listen for clues to discover their needs and desires.

Below is a basic template for your elevator speech. Fill in the blanks as applicable. Find their *why* or their pain and then provide the solution.

"Hello, my name is _____ and I help _____ like you do _____ and be able to _____."

How many people today will hear your elevator speech? Imagine the increase in your confidence and potential compensation when you do this once a day—or even three times a day—or ten. Optimize your time and talents to incorporate this into your daily routine, and strive to tell more and more people each day. Keep score, and compete with yourself. Make it fun, and remember to smile. You can achieve it!

Time, Talents and Treasures

Each person you meet has a different story. Each person joins Avon for a unique reason. What motivates you and gets you out of bed each morning? Focus on that *why* and devote your time to making it better.

As a leadership representative, be aware of and embrace the differences between your team members. As a sales representative, heed the same advice when servicing customers. Learn which fragrance to recommend based on listening to your customers' preferences. Let them know which skin care regimen is best for their skin type by paying careful attention to their lifestyle and concerns. Engage customers and team members in conversation by focusing on open-ended questions and listening to their responses. Master the skill of upselling, which is offering an additional product to complement the one ordered, or cross-category selling, which is offering a necklace to go with the perfume purchased.

Be yourself. Practice in front of a mirror. Have a pen and paper to write down someone's name and phone number after you share a brochure. Discover your strengths and stop your negative behaviors.

Reinvest the commissions you earn into building your business. Recommend your Avon services to each person who smiles at you until you reach the goal set for that hour. Repeat the process. Once you formulate the goals and navigate to achieve them, increase the amount of people you are reaching every day.

Promote, Promote, Promote

Being proactive means actively promoting the products, the opportunity and yourself. My friends tease me when we go out to a restaurant or take a road trip, because I am always an Avon lady.

I pass out business cards everywhere I go. If my car is parked, there are free brochures hanging from the windows for people parked near me. Car magnets stimulate interest in Avon while I am shopping in a store or visiting with a friend at the local coffee shop. Avon is part of me, and I promote it all the time, not just during "working" hours. Anytime, anywhere, always ask.

In the beginning, my confidence was low. I left brochures in random places, hoping people would find them and call me with orders. After getting slim results from that method, I decided that I needed to step outside my comfort zone daily. I initiated conversations about random topics to all kinds of different people. I would smile and offer brochures—and the calls started coming in.

Now, I pass out ten business cards every day—*the power of ten*. Whether I am talking to the cashier at a drive thru, secretary at the front desk, or a new neighbor, each day I go out and make contact with people. Be energetic and interesting. Hang brochures on the back window of your parked car as you run errands. Advertise your business on your car with magnets on your door panels or vinyl lettering on your windows. Once you make this an integral part of your daily routine, you will see your commission checks rise higher and higher. Infuse Avon into your daily life, rather than keeping it hidden in your pocket like a treasure no one should see.

Be Proactive and Partner with Uplifting People

Before I joined Avon, I was a regular customer for years. One day, my Avon lady said I could open up my own account if I still wanted Avon, because she was moving. She forwarded my name to a local manager, and an assistant came to my home to sign me up. Since I had only wanted to join Avon for a personal discount, she took a one-time $20 check for my placing a first product order. She missed out on the residual income earnings from the millions my team and I have sold over the years. This is a guiding force for me as an upline mentor. The Avon lady who moved away did not believe in investing her time and knowledge into making me a success. She took a few dollars and never looked back. Believe in yourself even if others do not.

Take Action to Succeed

How many hours a week do you invest in your business? As a leader, hold once-a-month unit meetings. As a sales representative, have skin care parties with your customers to increase commissions. Talk to three new people each day. Reward customers and team members with small tokens of appreciation. Be consistent with your efforts and the results will be abundant.

Avon has products for people who take a bath, shampoo their hair and have skin. Dispense the brochures and encourage online shoppers to place orders on your website. Consult with friends and family to get referrals for more clients. Schedule time to read motivational materials and educate yourself on the company's products and compensation plan.

Are you a believer and achiever? I believe in you and want you to achieve all the goals you desire and the dreams you deserve. Believe in yourself, in the company you represent, and in the products and opportunity you share. Be consistent and make a plan for each day to move your business to the next level. A talk show host once said, "Sometimes God whispers, and sometimes He throws a brick." Is this chapter your whisper, or your brick?

HEATHER MURRAY

Avon® Executive Unit Leader
Leader of Team Believe and Achieve
772-370-9060
avonmurray@yahoo.com
BUY: www.youravon.com/hmurray
SELL: www.startavon.com
using reference code HMURRAY

Heather graduated summa cum laude from West Chester University in Pennsylvania and moved to Florida to begin her career as an elementary school teacher. She joined Avon as a personal shopper and sold to friends and family. In 2006, Heather made Avon her sole career to be a stay-at-home mother.

Heather continued with Avon and expanded her leadership horizons, winning district awards. Making the switch from Avon being a hobby to a career also brought along other awards, beginning with Recruiting Excellence for 100+ recruits in 2006. Since then, Heather has received 17 other Avon leadership awards including #1 in Total Unit Sales Volume, #1 Total Unit Sales Increase, and #1 Downline Growth for the district. In 2013 she was awarded with #2 Division Downline Growth and received the Spirit of Avon award in 2008 and 2012.

Heather and her husband, Sean, have three beautiful daughters. Running an Avon business has provided income and the flexibility to attend therapy sessions with their special needs child. Heather volunteers for the nursery and is on the core team for the children's ministry at Vero Christian Church.

Flying with the Eagles

BY MALCOLM AND MARY SHELTON

Growing up as one of eight sons of tenant farmers in the Alta Vista area of Virginia, I never once thought of Avon®, much less of being an Avon representative. I was the fourth son, born in 1934. Tobacco was our crop and I learned to pull, cure and take it to market. While none of us brothers felt drawn to being farmers, we all learned that hard work and the American dream would give us a healthy and comfortable lifestyle, which we all achieved!

At 18 I left the farm, married, and raised four beautiful daughters. We lived in Charlottesville, Norfolk and Virginia Beach, with some time in Springfield, Missouri. I was an auto mechanic and progressed to selling car diagnostic equipment. However, my entrepreneurial spirit, which I realized started in my youth when I trapped and skinned rabbits for extra income, really came alive when I discovered network marketing. I achieved a fair amount of success with a number of companies, but they folded on me.

The Avon Connection

I met and married Mary seven years after my first marriage ended. I continued to find other network marketing companies, none of which lasted long. While attending yet another opportunity meeting, my host commented, "Amway® thinks they are number one in network marketing, but Avon is the real number one." I knew nothing about Avon, yet that comment kept ringing in my head. I had seen an Avon ad in our local paper, and this time I called it. I had a 45-minute phone call with Sandra Bell. In July 1993, Mary and I joined Avon. I was 59 and wondering if I would ever find lasting success as an entrepreneur.

I watched one Virginia Beach district manager induct someone into Avon and took off on my own for the rest of them. I hit it hard, gave up the last of my menial jobs (stocking shelves at the commissary) and decided to focus on Avon full time. For me that meant eight- to ten-hour days flat out, while Mary brought in the dependable check that paid the bills.

Sandra and I developed an effective system. She continued to take the calls from the ads and relay them back to me (before cell phones). I met with each person and at one stretch brought 100 people into Avon in 90 days. Some of those early reps are still with us, the most notable being Dayna Chandler.

I developed sales by passing out 500 brochures each campaign, focusing on businesses. I added a dedicated fax machine line to our home office and frequently found orders on the fax machine when I came home from "Avoning."

I soon realized that the best money to be made in Avon was in leadership. I decided that I would become a Senior Executive Unit Leader and did so in 18 months.

Mary's Story

Malcolm and I met at Toastmasters®, an organization dedicated to improving public speaking and leadership skills. That was 1987 in Norfolk, Virginia. I had been on the other side of a divorce for 14 years and had no children. Malcolm and I married less than a year later. We moved into our new apartment with no furniture. We asked friends for their cast-offs and quickly filled our small home. I realized that Malcolm was not bringing much of an income into our life; therefore, I switched from a job with Norfolk Public Schools to a better-paying one with Virginia Beach Public Library.

I knew a bit about network marketing. As a single woman, I had avoided the inevitable invitation to join Amway. However, shortly after marrying Malcolm, we gave Amway a try. A few other opportunities come along, and I did find a couple of them exciting. Malcolm was the prime mover through all of them, and I tried to be supportive.

When he joined Avon, he described the leadership program to me. I said, "Please, not another network marketing venture. Sell that Skin So Soft®, but please, not the leadership thing." I must say I am thankful he did not listen to me.

Sometime after he gained confidence in Avon, he said, "One day I'll earn as much with Avon as you're earning now." By this time I had transitioned to the public school and was on the masters pay schedule. I replied, "Great! Do that! In fact, if you double my income, I'll leave my job." Four years later he did just that! I gladly took an early retirement at age 56.

Back to Malcolm: The Birth of the Mighty Eagles

I wanted a name for our team that was more exciting than the

Shelton Team. I enjoyed the movie *The Mighty Ducks,* but felt that "ducks" might not be inspiring; hence, the Mighty Eagles. I created our motto as our annual conferences began. We opened each one with: *We are the Mighty Eagles. We see further, fly faster, and soar higher. We are the Mighty Eagles.* Try an exciting name and "chant" for your team. It creates fantastic energy at the start of a meeting, on Facebook and in emails!

Working Avon as a couple!

We had progressed to a lovey home in Chesapeake by the time Mary joined me full time in Avon. We did newsletters to our team members, mailing them out long before the Internet allowed e-newsletters. We had an annual gathering of our team at the oceanfront in Virginia Beach in January, when hotel rooms were more affordable. Team members came from Asheville and eastern North Carolina, Savannah, Georgia and parts of Virginia. At the time, with leadership being a new phenomenon in Avon, district and division managers wanted to attend our annual weekend conference to check us out. I guess we met with their approval, as no one ever corrected our procedures or content.

Lisa Wilber, one of our upline, came to Virginia a number of times to speak to our team and encourage both sales and leadership in ways that might stretch comfort zones!

The annual conferences lasted about 10 years, ending in 2005, when attendance did not justify continuing. We now travel as guest speakers and encouragers to our various teams when they meet. This seems to work best for our scattered team. We now have groups in Virginia Beach, North Carolina, Savannah, Pennsylvania and Minnesota.

Use Your Upline

Sandra Bell and Lisa Wilber were instrumental in the growth of the Mighty Eagles, each in her own special way. We have passed that same support along to our team members. We serve as guest speakers at team member meetings. One-on-one support is equally important. Occasionally a member has a challenge with Avon's customer care, a district manager, or another representative. Inspired by Sarah Palin, Mary calls this being a "momma grizzly." Joining a representative in such a battle shows her that you are truly in her corner. Just be sure to hear both sides of the story before getting too worked up.

The battle can become more serious when a policy decision from Avon threatens to impact representatives' business success. Executives and Senior Executives can speak for a large number of representatives. Avon knows this and will listen. If an issue grips your heart, you can believe it grips the heart of many on your team. Speak up to the right people in Avon as an individual, using "I" since you probably did not survey your team to gather a consensus. Then add your title to your signature. Therein lies your power. We owe this to our team members. Initiate a call to your upline as needed. Remember, she is earning money from Avon on your efforts. Do not hesitate to ask for help or information. You are not "interrupting" her work. You are her work. Most of us tell our team members, "Call when you need me." Take her at her word and call!

Recognition in Many Forms

Not everyone needs to see her name in lights at a ball game. Some people are truly upset when people sing Happy Birthday to them in a restaurant. There is no one type of recognition that will suit all your team members. We have all heard so many wonderful recognition ideas. Facebook and other social media currently provide the most popular platforms.

Here are some we have used:

- Best seller each campaign gets Starbucks® hour with team leader
- Top sellers listed for all to see (variety of formats – your choice!)
- Anniversary and birthday cards through Downline Manager
- Gift packets awarded to those who are celebrating five years or more with Avon
- Postcards to five different people each campaign, patting them on the back for some specific accomplishment
- Cash gift to those who achieve a particular Avon incentive

Where Does the Money Go?

When I joined Avon, I scraped together $250 to pay for one month of newspaper ads. After that, the business paid for itself. I reinvested every penny from leadership into the business. Recognition, incentives, office equipment, meeting expenses and travel were covered by Avon checks. It was not until the third year that I allowed leadership checks to be used for personal items. The fourth year, we moved to a new home and indulged in a new car.

This took discipline. We see many representatives spending their business money on personal things rather than investing in the business. Then they wonder why their team is not growing. We advise using sales commission for personal expenses and leadership for reinvestment in your business, even when the check is $25.

I will admit to some extravagance once the income exceeded the necessary business outgo. There was an airplane and an RV. I learned from those experiences and have grown beyond them. If you have squandered money, do not beat yourself up—or your spouse. Learn and grow. John Maxwell calls it "failing forward." Determining what went wrong and why, and then strategizing how to prevent that mistake in the future can carry you through lots of grief and allow you to be successful.

Now in our senior years, we have down-sized our home and our "stuff." We are both blessed with the gift of giving to Christian charities. We keep our list of charities short because we believe it is better to give more to a few than smaller amounts to many. Thinking of that encourages us as we walk through a store to say, "Look at all the stuff we don't need."

Staying in good health is also a current expenditure. We are exploring alternative or integrative medicine to free us from prescription drugs and set a new, age-gracefully model.

Men in Avon

I've learned that I am a rarity in Avon. The ribbing I experienced when I gave brochures to men in their auto shops could have been discouraging. Very few men see the opportunity in Avon and decide to go for it. Many who are successful now actually discovered Avon when they saw the money their wives were making.

Women frequently ask me, "How can I get my husband involved in Avon?" The obvious answer, "Show him the money," does not work for many women new to leadership because there is very little money to show. They say, "There would be more money if he helped me."

Take a good look at your husband's skills, interests and commitments. There may be ways he can help, short of a full-time involvement.
• Take care of children, shopping or cooking to free up your time
• Handle computer work

- Make phone calls
- Unpack orders, organize products or make deliveries
- Track income and expenses for taxes

Mary and I have different skills and personalities that we have blended into the business to be most effective. She is the organizer and computer operator. I did not have the courage to face a computer until I was seventy. I am the intuitive type who finds new ways of developing the business and working with representatives to help them realize their goals. Nitty-gritty details drain my energy while Mary thrives on them. I am spontaneous by nature while Mary is structured. Once we learned to appreciate our differences instead of fighting them, we discovered harmony.

Onward and Upward

Advice on how to build your Avon business is plentiful. Since we each learn in different ways, consider help in the forms most appealing to you, and then push out of your comfort zone to try some of the others. Here are some valuable sources:

- Avon's Pathways
- Conference calls from Avon's division, district managers and staff
- District and team meetings, rallies, national conferences
- Outside sources: leadership training seminars, Toastmasters, Dale Carnegie® and adult education programs in your community
- Books and magazines
- Motivational CDs in your car (much more beneficial than news and music)
- Prospecting with your team members or district manager
- Talking to everyone about Avon
- Wearing Avon buttons or nametags
- And the real biggie: *persistence*

We have seen so many representatives come and go. They do not catch the vision, the money is not enough or immediate enough, they do not want to invest time and energy, or "Johnny has a cold." A truism I have learned is: *Any excuse will do when you don't want to do something.*

If you set your goals, work the step-by-step path toward them and enjoy the journey, you will find the satisfaction and benefits of being an Avon success!

MALCOLM AND MARY SHELTON
Avon® Senior Executive Unit Leader
The Mighty Eagles Team

336-447-4754
avonsuccess@mshelton.net
www.youravon.com/mshelton

Malcolm gained experience with life and people first on the farm, then in auto shops, and finally in network marketing. He tried many companies before choosing Avon®. Now celebrating 21 years with Avon and 26 years with Mary, he is enjoying the time and financial freedom Avon provides.

Malcolm and Mary attended their first Avon National Recognition Event in 1995 in New Orleans. They were hooked and qualified for "two free" every year since then. They enjoy traveling and especially embrace the challenge of adding to their Avon trips by blending business with pleasure. Their favorite trip was a cross-country drive from Chesapeake, Virginia, to San Diego, California. They took 11 days to get to the Pacific Ocean and spent 1 month getting back to the Atlantic.

Malcolm has met the challenge of starting two daughters, one granddaughter and a brother in Avon. His daughter Wanda Jackson is the best achiever with twenty years of Avon, consistently at President's Club or higher.

As a final word of wisdom, Malcolm has learned from Jim Rohn, American motivational speaker, that "profits are better than wages."

Creative Selling

BY DOLLY AND HENRY ASPEYTIA

I was born and raised in Chula Vista, California, a part of San Diego County. I was the oldest daughter of five children. My mother was a housewife and my father worked in the construction field as a plasterer. He worked Monday through Friday from sunup to sundown.

Every night, when my father arrived home from work, dinner was always ready and we sat down together as a family. My hardworking father provided for all of our needs, and I truly believe that a part of what drives me to work so hard today is growing up with his hardworking example.

We were very much a Mexican-American family. My siblings and I did not speak Spanish at all. It was not necessary, as our parents and our nana and tata already spoke English. We held Mexican traditions and values, yet were very much American. For example, we always had a piñata for birthdays and tamales for Christmas. Family members were always together and the atmosphere was like a large, loud party.

When we went to church, the services were held in Spanish, so I understood just a little. I was extremely shy. I would not participate in conversation and my long, brown hair would cover my face. I had no close friends, and that was okay with me. I spent many hours alone in my room listening to the radio. I knew the words to every song and sang along. Because of my shyness, I would refuse to do oral reports and would rather receive an "F" than stand in front of the class and read aloud.

My family never spoke of higher education. It was expected that when I reached adulthood, my job would be to marry and have children. I wondered how I would be able to do that when I was so shy.

Opposites Attract

Henry, my husband, was raised in a Christian family. When we met, he was devoted to church work, serving as a youth and children's minister. It has been said that "opposites attract." This was so true in our case. He was not at all shy. Henry had not found a microphone he did not like! He had no problem speaking to large audiences.

Henry and I share a mutual, yet different, love for music. While he directed the choir, I stood in the back row of the Alto section. We began dating shortly after we met, and were married one and a half years later.

I signed up with a direct sales company that was primarily a party plan business. Because of my shyness, I would conveniently schedule the parties for when I was supposed to be at work. Henry would graciously step up and take my place. I lasted long enough to fill my cupboards with plastic containers.

Checking Out Avon

About one year into our marriage, we wanted to start a family. I told Henry I did not want to raise our children in an apartment; however, our part-time wages were not enough to purchase or rent a house in San Diego. God made a way, through answered prayer, for us to relocate to Dallas, Texas. We were both offered full-time employment, which afforded us the opportunity to purchase a house and start our family. Within a year we were welcoming our firstborn, Joshua Henry, into the family.

I decided to give Avon a try. I called the company and the district sales manager came out to get me started. I was given a territory in my neighborhood. I went door to door, and no one was home, so I left brochures on the doors. I received one phone call and an order. I attended one sales meeting.

I asked the women at the church I was attending if they would be interested in receiving a brochure and ordering. Unfortunately, they already had an Avon representative they were ordering from. When it came time to deliver the only order I received, the customer had moved and had not left a forwarding address. I lasted only one month in the new business before I decided it was not for me.

Sylvia and Jonathan were the blessings that completed our family. When Jonathan was six months old, we returned to the San Diego area. My heart was always there. I wanted something to do and thought of Avon. Again I called, and the manager came out to get me started. I received a big binder with information on all the products. This time I was determined to make it work and read the entire binder.

My first order consisted of lots of samples because I wanted to be prepared. I presented my brochures to my church family and my natural family and got little response. The noes really hurt. That is when I decided to ask strangers, and that did not hurt as much. Living in an area that was primarily Spanish speaking, I began to reach out to my community. They accepted me with open arms. Before I knew it, I was speaking Spanish myself. When necessity and opportunity meet, magic happens!

Attending sales meetings and using the product gave me confidence. I quickly made President's Club, and Avon recognized my achievements. The leadership program was introduced, and I got on board. There were several of us in the area who participated, and we grew together. We did not know what we were doing; however, we believed in what we were doing and just shared our love for the product.

An opening for District Sales Manager (DSM) came up and my manager thought of me. Although I was flattered when she presented the opportunity, I did not believe it was for me. Henry encouraged me to go for it saying, "If you did get the job and didn't like it, you could always quit." He did not want me to have regrets about passing up the opportunity.

I did become a DSM and learned so much during those three years. Among the things I learned were planning, commitment and dedication. I longed for free time, and having three children made it hard to attend their events.

A New Focus

Henry and I had a heart-to-heart discussion. We agreed that I could use what I learned as a manager, put in a third of the time, and succeed as a leadership representative. I gave my notice and signed up as an Independent Sales Representative, with Henry as my co-applicant. We were on our way to Senior Executive Unit Leader (SEUL).

"Successful people do what unsuccessful people are not willing to do, and that often means living outside the limits of one's comfort zone."
—Jeff Olson, American sales and leadership trainer, public speaker and founder of livehappy.com

Right away I approached a local mercado and asked if I could set up at the entrance. The manager agreed to $25 per day, for as many hours as I wanted. I was there two days a week for four to six hours. I stood behind a table with Avon brochures and a raffle basket, getting names and signing up representatives. I worked outside the mercado for two months straight. My upline, Gaye Costa, supported me with materials like brochures and samples. I achieved Unit Leader within the first two months and received a $100 bonus.

I continued to set up tables and go to street fairs, inviting my downline to join me whenever possible. I knew that we would have potential customers who would need service, and I had representatives who wanted the extra opportunity. People showed interest in earning extra money with Avon. When they saw the potential for growth in leadership, it was easier to get them on board. At these venues, it was all about making a connection.

I would rather get 10 names with connections than 100 names with no connections. It is important to know names and even more valuable to learn details about each person. Are they married? Do they have children? Do they work? What are some of their short-term goals? In a short conversation, I can find out that "Brenda" has two children, who are starting school soon, and that she needs extra money for school clothes.

It took me six months to get to AUL, four years to get to EUL, and seven years to get to SEUL. Sure, my goal was to advance more quickly. What is nice about this business, however, is that even when I do not achieve a goal, I am always closer than I was when I started.

I grew as my team grew. We were like a family, with the majority of us living within 30 minutes of our training center, which became a place where we would meet up and visit. We often had get-togethers, which included food and prizes—a little business and a little pleasure. We always made sure that whatever we were doing was fun.

> *"I did it my way."*
> **—Frank Sinatra, American singer,**
> **actor and filmmaker**

Planning for Success

I set a day aside for planning and reflection. Avon's ninety-day business plan has always worked for me. When you fill it out, you can see if there has been growth in your business or not. It has always been a goal of mine to grow. Once I have written my three-month plan, I review each campaign to see if I need to make adjustments.

Small, bite-size pieces work for me. I constantly keep myself on task by committing to the plan. I review each campaign once it has closed and plan events accordingly. My calendar is always close by. If it is empty, that means I am not working my plan. When it comes to my planner, I make it a point to put family first, then spirituality, then Avon.

I am in communication with my first generation leaders on at least a monthly basis, some as often as two times a week. They know that I am available for questions or clarification when it comes to incentives, or policy and procedure.

Recognition is important. I have a private Facebook® page where I recognize the top ten in sales, sales leadership and recruiting. From time to time, I send out gift cards from Target®, See's®, or Chick-fil-A® to the number one achievers in these categories.

I am constantly putting new representatives to work. I make myself available to them for shadowing. If they want to have a table somewhere, I will go out with them to show how I interact with potential customers or recruits. Modeling is extremely important. I am a visual person, and this is the best way I learn.

Stay Positive!

Sometimes it is not easy to be positive when you schedule appointments that turn out to be no-shows, or when you help with an open house and the new representative does not follow up or show up, or when you do not requalify for your current title status. Try to find the positive in everything. Use that extra time to make phone calls, train a new representative, or take time for reflection. I have become very creative when it comes to finding the positive—and it works.

Making time for yourself is important. Singing Gospel music is one of our loves. Henry and I have been part of the San Diego Multicultural Gospel Choir for several years, and even though we have moved out of the area, we are still called back for special events.

I also volunteered to do crisis intervention with the Citizens Adversity Support Team, or CAST, in Chula Vista, California. I believe that when we help others, we not only do a service for them, we also help ourselves. Sometimes our issues are so small compared to those of others.

Henry and I also give to Music for Purpose, a free music program in Vista, California. We are involved in Perfume Worship, a live CD recording, the proceeds of which go toward building a music program for orphans in Honduras.

Now that Henry has retired, a lot of the little things can get done. I am so grateful to have someone who can help me in the big and little things. At first he helped by bringing in the boxes with my orders, loading and unloading. Now he is great about meeting people and sharing the Avon opportunity with them. Henry has also helped with motivating the team, which consists of 800 representatives in 22 states. Of those representatives, 35 are title leaders, and we have 29 candidates. Last cycle we sold $2.5 million.

We have been able to travel quite a bit because of Avon. We have been to the Bahamas, Jamaica, Hawaii, Puerto Rico, and on a Caribbean cruise. Joshua and Sylvia have received bachelor's degrees thanks to Avon. Our youngest, Jonathan, is attending college as we write this. I now drive my dream car—a 2013 BMW 328i.

> *"Don't Stop Believing."*
> **—Journey, American rock band**

We still have goals and dreams. We would like to take my parents to Hawaii, remodel our home in San Diego, and become NSEULs. I want to continue to step out of my comfort zone and experience life in a whole new way. I have gotten braver and take more risks, because now I know that if it does not work out, at least I tried. I used to be afraid to fail; therefore, I did not try. Now I fear almost nothing. My greatest fear is… What if…?

> *"I can do all things through Christ which strengthens me."*
> **—Phil 4:13**

> *"The only place where success comes before work*
> *is in the dictionary."*
> **—Vidal Sassoon, British hairdresser,**
> **businessman, and philanthropist**

Success is our destination and there are many roads to get there. What worked for me might not work for you. Find your own method of success. Follow these directions on your map to your dreams:

Embrace commitment. Be willing to put in time and energy. Get support and encouragement from people close to you. Persevere, even if it seems the effort is not paying off.

Make a plan. Meet with your upline and/or manager. Make a ninety-day plan and a year plan. Work your ninety-day plan in thirty-day increments. Schedule events to help you reach your goals. Remember to schedule family time and anything else important to you.

Work your plan. Be consistent. Review each week and recognize your achievement and opportunity for growth. Reward yourself and your support group—family, close friends, team members—for milestones. Be proud out loud!

DOLLY AND HENRY ASPEYTIA
Avon® Senior Executive Unit Leaders

619-428-9777
hellodollya@hotmail.com
www.youravon.com/daspeytia

Dolly and Henry were both born in San Diego, California, and raised in Christian homes with strong family values. They were married in 1981 and have since raised three wonderful children.

They have consistently supported each other's endeavors. Along the way, Dolly has been awarded the "Spirit of Avon" twice. Her leaders consider her to be a great friend and mentor. She has helped many women achieve a better life through her unwavering dedication.

Dolly's success has enabled Henry to retire early from the electrical trade and pursue his dream of coaching high school track. Family time is always number one on their calendar, and they love to travel. They reside in Tempe, Arizona. They have four grand doggies: Yoshi, Kanti, Guapo and Kyuubi.

Planning the Journey of a Lifetime

BY DILENIA COLLADO

I was born in the Dominican Republic. When I was only five years old, my mother brought my younger sister, Maria, and I to the United States where we settled in New York. Living here was not easy, because my mother did not speak any English. When we were very young, my sister and I had to help her with almost everything that had to do with translating papers, including our school-related forms.

My mother worked two jobs to take care of us. Starting as early as junior high school, I decided I wanted to help her with the bills by finding my own job. Maria and I dreamed of doing better with our lives. She wanted to be a doctor and I wanted to be a lawyer.

After starting high school, I lost my focus and did not know where my life was heading. I got married after graduating and had my first son at the age of 19.

I worked a full-time job as a customer service representative for a printing company and felt the need for more. I decided to go back to school, yet I did not know exactly what I wanted to study. I could only attend school part time because I had a young son to care for and still needed to work my full-time job. We needed to have two incomes in my household.

Two years after starting college to become a certified public accountant, I found out I was pregnant with our second child. Wow! How things were going to change for me now. I had to put my college career on standby until my daughter was born.

When I was seven months pregnant, I met Dorothy, a real estate broker who was a good friend of my husband's. She said that I had a great personality and that I was very friendly. She suggested that I try taking the real estate test and start working for her. I took the course, passed the New York state exam in 1996, and began working for Dorothy.

At that time, the real estate market was doing well. Unfortunately, the market dropped in 2005, and I needed to go back to work at a regular job. I returned to the printing industry because that was what I knew best. Soon after that, my marriage ended and I became a single mom. It seemed I was repeating my mother's story. I moved back to my hometown, where most of my family lived. I struggled month to month to make ends meet and managed to keep my head above water.

A Silver Lining Appears

When my daughter Karina was 14, she asked me if she could get a job. She wanted to be able to buy the things that a parent with only one income could not afford to buy her. My response was no. I told her she needed to focus on her schoolwork and get good grades. For the next two weeks, all our conversations focused on Karina wanting a job. Trying to discourage a teenager from getting a job was very difficult.

One day, we saw an Avon® commercial. I asked Karina if she wanted to sell Avon. She was under 18, and therefore not allowed to sign up; however, we agreed that I would sign up for her. I helped Karina sell at my job and to family and friends. After selling for two months, she decided that she did not want to continue selling Avon. I had several customers already and loved the Avon products myself, so I made the decision to continue selling.

Enjoying Lifestyle Perks

After exploring several opportunities and careers options, I was interested in the possibility of making my own hours and devoting time to business as well as family and friends. I put my best foot forward and started to enjoy the endless possibilities that Avon could offer me.

Avon has given me the opportunity to start a wonderful life journey. I earned my first trip to Las Vegas and was able to be a guest at the yearly Senior Executive Unit Leader (SEUL) trips to Hawaii and Puerto Rico. Thanks to the flexibility of having my own Avon business, I have taken many other family trips. I would not have been able to take the time off for those if I had been working a regular nine-to-five job.

Personal Growth

In the past, I was too shy to do any public speaking. In 2012 I was invited, along with my upline, to speak at the Avon annual event in

Foxwoods. First we told our story in front of about three hundred Avon leaders. Then we were asked to speak in front of 2,000 representatives. I was terrified and nervous and did it anyway. After that experience, I can say I am no longer afraid to speak in public. Those who know me now would never believe I was a shy person at one time, because now I cannot stop talking about my career decision!

Life-changing Experiences

Avon has changed the way I think as a person and a business owner. On the trip to Puerto Rico, I had a blast, and it was a wonderful experience. I hung out at the pool and the beach every morning while talking to the top sellers and SEULs of Avon. I asked many questions and gained plenty of ideas to better my business.

To this day, I often look back at an experience I had at the casino in Puerto Rico. I love playing cards and roulette. During one of the first nights at the casino, I decided to play roulette. I was having a great time hitting a few numbers and winning a little when a couple of Hispanic Avon representatives came to my table. We started making noise, calling out numbers, and having a great time. The following evening, I met back at the table with the same representatives. Again, we had a blast and laughed the night away.

The next evening, we attended the Avon Gala Dinner. The event started off with recognitions. I was so excited to see all the new faces of the people who were going to get awarded for their efforts during the previous year. To my surprise, when they announced the 2013 Woman of Enterprise, and she started walking up to the stage, my mouth dropped to the floor. I could not believe my eyes. It was one of the representatives I had played roulette with the past two nights. I could not hold back the tears as she turned to me and smiled. Wow!

She was a regular person just like me. Her speech was so emotional and motivating that I told myself, *one day, that will be me.*

Hard Work Pays Off

Start by setting a goal, and plan how you will achieve it. I planned and achieved my goal in a short time. I started selling Avon in June of 2010. One day, I received an email from a lady named Maria, and she said that I was number ten in sales on her team for that given campaign. I called my upline and asked her who Maria Tirotta was, and she said that Maria was my great-grandmother in Avon. I said, "Okay good, but I want to be number one."

Being recognized by Maria was the best thing that could have happened to me at that moment. I made it a point to sell more and more every campaign until I finally made number one. I wanted to prove that I could do more, and I did; I made President's Club by that December and Honor Society in my first year.

Multilingual Skills Lead to Leadership

My first award with Avon was Best New Performer at the annual President's Club Tribute. My upline, Laura Douglas-Robinson, called me consistently about moving my Avon business to the next level. She wanted me to start doing leadership. I kept refusing her offer because I was happy with what I was making and had no time due to my full-time job. One day, Laura called and asked me for a favor. She wanted me to accompany her to an appointment with a young lady who was more comfortable speaking Spanish. Laura needed me to translate for her, and I was happy to do so. After the appointment, having gained new information, I asked Laura if that was all I needed to do to start my leadership business, and her response was yes.

I wanted to learn as much as I could. I took all the training classes Avon offered online and also attended every meeting and event. At my district meeting, I learned that not everyone is working their Avon business to its full potential. I decided to make sure that I was one of the many people who would go on to make Avon a full-time career. After analyzing how much money I was making selling the Avon products and the potential money I could be making starting leadership, I decided it was time to quit my job.

I was scared and nervous. There was no turning back. Avon was it for me. I was determined to make a living and pay my bills with my business income. I called Laura and told her that I wanted to make a plan and that my goal was to make Executive Unit Leader (EUL) by campaign 7 of 2012.

Making a Plan and Sticking to It

I started my plan in mid-November of 2011 on Long Island, New York, where it was very cold, but that was not going to stop me. Every morning, seven days a week, Laura and I would meet for breakfast and plan our day. Some days turned into nights. By campaign 3, I made Advanced Unit Leader and continued with my daily routine. I made sure that I called everyone in my first generation and told them what I was doing and where I was recruiting, in case they wanted to join me. A few representatives did join me.

Although I had to travel abroad for two weeks, interrupting my routine, I was still determined to make my goal once I returned to the United States. I just had to work in a shorter time frame than I had planned. By campaign 7 of 2012, I met my goal and titled as Executive Unit Leader (EUL). Determination paid off.

Once you set a goal, do not let anything stop you—not the weather, not people and not circumstances. My motivation was bolstered once I started to see the fruit of my labor. I also found it very rewarding to meet new people and steer them in the right direction.

Starting an Avon career gave a lot of my sales representatives a job and motivation to improve their lives. After signing up new representatives, I consider them my friends. We are on the same team, and I encourage them to do better by providing them with tips and ideas of how to make more money. Now my task is to teach all my new representatives to do the same as I have done. I am still struggling to find my next EUL, and I am not giving up hope. One day, someone will want it and will work as hard as I did to get it.

Stay Focused on Your Goal

- Analyze every incentive Avon has to offer and go for it.
- Call the leaders and representatives consistently to let them know that you have not forgotten about them.
- Recognize your team members every campaign.
- Put together team incentives.
- Set up recruiting events. Invite leaders and non-leaders to join.
- Do not give up.

My new goal is to make Senior Executive Unit Leader. I am planning it and will make it. I am in search of the right person to come along whom I can help while concurrently making my way to SEUL. I am not giving up. Every time I feel discouraged, I remember all the trips and awards I have received from Avon. I think of all the wonderful people who were just like me. If they did it, I can too. The words of wisdom and encouragement I have received from all those top SEUL representatives are stuck in my mind.

Also, be true to yourself and those around you. Set a goal today. It does not have to be a fast-paced one. Then plan how you are going to get to that goal and stick to the plan. When things in life do not go according to plan, you have to get up and start all over. Never give up on your dreams and goals. One day you will see them come true.

DILENIA COLLADO
Avon® Executive Unit Leader

516-852-0246
dileniacollado@yahoo.com
www.youravon.com/dcollado

Dilenia was born in the Dominican Republic and speaks both Spanish and English fluently. She is the oldest of seven children. Today she lives in Freeport, New York on Long Island. Dilenia worked in the printing industry for over twenty years as a customer service representative and also a printing manger. She has been a licensed real estate broker since 1996.

Dilenia decided to start her own business in 2010 and is proud to see her Avon business grow. She is an Executive Unit Leader (EUL), a David H. McConnell member and a Certified Beauty Advisor. Dilenia realized early on that helping others was in her nature. She is a team player and is always determined to help others. Dilenia set a goal to make EUL, worked hard to achieve it, and went from Unit Leader to Executive Unit Leader in four campaigns. She will never stop dreaming!

Dilenia is a single parent of two wonderful kids, Luis and Karina. She likes to dance, play Bingo and take family vacations with her kids.

Overcoming Obstacles
Especially When that Obstacle is YOU

BY JENNETT CENNAME PULLEY

I always tell potential new business partners that I am no one special; I am simply a mom, a wife and an Avon® lady. I do not know the meaning of life or have all the magic answers. I am only an expert on my own little world and strive to do the best I can. I have clear-cut ideas of where I want to be and focus on what will help me reach my goals. Like most people, I often stumble along the way; however, I refuse to fail. The only way I can lose is if I choose to stop trying, and that is not an option. I truly believe that anyone can do what I do. They just need to decide to do so.

EEEK! I'm an Adult. Now What?

I graduated from Virginia Commonwealth University in May 1995 with degrees in psychology and public relations. I became a training manager for a large telecommunications company—a job I loved. The hours were erratic and there was a lot of travel, but my husband

and I had just married and purchased our first home, and the money was great.

When my husband and I decided to start a family, I thought I wanted to maintain my career in the corporate world. However, that quickly changed once I had to drop off my babies at daycare every day. My "ah ha" moment came one afternoon as I was picking up my children from our sitter's house. After buckling them into the car, I sat in the driveway and sobbed about all the moments I had missed with them during the day. I knew then that the corporate world was no longer what I wanted. A change was in order.

I still needed an income. While my husband had a great job, I did not want to put the full burden of our finances on him. Plus, I loved spending money. I was fortunate enough to be able to take a buy-out from my employer. I paid off all my debt and put a few months worth of salary in the bank while I figured out what I wanted to do.

My first plan was to babysit in my home. The problem was that I am not a big fan of other people's kids. I also wanted to enjoy outings with my own sweet girls. The responsibility of running a daycare was more than I wanted to handle. I did not want to work nights, weekends and holidays in retail. There were not many other options for a young mother of two that would give me the flexibility I desired. Many of my friends who were also stay-at-home moms had ventured into the direct marketing world. This sounded interesting because I loved the idea of being my own boss.

Why Avon?

I started my Avon business in July 2001. I chose the company because I was not interested in the party plan most other home-based businesses used. With no quotas or inventory and the low start-up fee of $10, I had nothing to lose. I knew my chances of repeat business were excellent as long as I provided great customer service and made myself the Avon lady in the area.

Like many women I meet in Avon, I ran into a lot of naysayers. People said that direct marketing was a "pyramid scheme," that no one made money, or that I would be in debt within a month. Someone even told me to just roll down the car window and throw out my $10 because it would be faster. I was highly competitive and more than willing to work tirelessly to prove the doubters wrong.

Discover Your Whys

My goal was to stay home with my children while still earning enough money to live comfortably. I did not want to work a "real job" on someone else's schedule. I did not want to miss a field trip, doctor's appointment or class party. I wanted to be "that mom" who could volunteer at a moment's notice and who knew all the kids' friends. I wanted to have time to make a difference in someone else's life. I also wanted to avoid financial stress in my happy marriage.

I needed to earn $500 a month to make ends meet. Every time I left the house, I reminded myself that I needed to talk to at least three people about my Avon business or I would end up back in a business suit, commuting to work. With Avon, I could take my kids to work with me, and I did not have to wear heels or hose.

One of the most valuable lessons you can learn when starting a new endeavor is that it is imperative to figure out why you are doing it. Having clarity on your ultimate goal for your business gives you an anchor to hold onto when things are rocky. It is also important to celebrate your successes along the way.

"It's not who you are underneath. It's what you do that defines you."
—**Bruce Wayne,** ***Batman Begins,*** **2005**

But I'm Shy

I started out very hesitant to approach people about my business. I still had the baby weight, I lived across town from my closest friends, and I was terribly afraid of rejection. I lacked the self-confidence that other moms seemed to have. They all seemed so well put together, and I felt lost.

The naysayers did a great job of planting seeds of doubt. As determined as I was to prove them wrong, I still heard their voices whenever I talked to someone about Avon. I had no upline to guide me. Fortunately, I quickly realized that my excuses would be my biggest obstacles if I allowed them to be. I needed to find my way on my own.

My *whys* were my answer and my strength. Whenever self-doubt would creep in and try to stop me from opening my mouth, I would reflect back on that day sitting in the driveway at the sitter's house and remind myself why I became an Avon lady. There was nothing more important to me, and that awareness is what has led to my success. That motivated me to earn Rose Circle during my first year with Avon.

But I'm Not a Salesperson

Eventually, I realized I wanted to help other women—and a few great men—realize their dreams with Avon. I knew that if I could succeed with my sales business, I could help others do the same. With the valuable training skills I had learned in my corporate job, I started a team. The most common objection I have heard from both men and women is, "But I'm not a salesperson."

The fact is, you use sales skills in your everyday life. Whether you are making a first impression on someone you just met, describing a favorite movie to a friend, convincing your children to eat their veggies, or sweet-talking your spouse into taking out the trash, you are selling an idea or opinion. All you have to do is transfer those skills to selling product or opportunity.

In order to be a great salesperson or consultant, you must find your passion. Do you love skincare or helping others find their confidence through color? Do you know someone who is not mobile and would benefit from shopping from home? Do you know someone who needs to make purchases on a budget? If you can focus on what you love about the company you represent and what uniqueness you bring, you can share that love with others. People will recognize your passion and mirror it back to you in the form of sales.

I Don't Want to Be Pushy

You do not need to be pushy to be successful. When I started my business, I cringed at the thought of my friends or family dreading being around me, wondering if I was going to push my product on them. I never wanted them to feel uncomfortable using a competitor's product. I did not want them to worry that I would continuously try to recruit them into my opportunity. My fear led me to the other extreme. I never mentioned my business or offered a brochure. Big mistake—it is possible to find a middle ground.

I succeeded by building trust with each potential customer or team member. It is crucial to make your business about her, not about you. The old adage that says you were given two ears and one mouth for a reason—is true. The key to being successful in sales and leadership is active listening. People like to be heard and understood. Giving them the floor makes you the best conversationalist in town.

Discover her needs and desires, whether it be skincare, because she does not wear makeup, jewelry to freshen her wardrobe, or more money in her budget. Ask questions and show how you can help her fulfill her needs with your products or opportunity. When you focus on what she wants instead of what you can sell her, your business thrives and you gain her loyalty and trust. Asking her for referrals is then easy, and she will be thrilled to tell her friends about you.

I Need a Real Job

I love to participate in job fairs. They are a great chance to share my non-traditional opportunity with those who need to earn money. At every event, I hear the objection, "I need a real job." It is all I can do not to point out which side of the table I am standing on.

With my "not real" job, I am the boss. I decide my hours and daily activities. I decide which team members to reward and which to give extra attention to. I get to be creative with how to promote my business and myself. I decide when to sit back and re-evaluate and when to work harder.

Most important, I am in charge of my paycheck. No waiting for an annual raise that does not even cover a tank of gas. I get to decide if I get a bonus or earn the company vacation. I choose the incentives I want and how to earn them.

It is not always easy. Sometimes I lose my way. When I stumble, I have no one to blame but myself. When I succeed, I get to take all the credit. I love my "not real" job, and I really love my boss.

There Is Not Enough Time in the Day

No, there is not enough time in the day to do everything you want to do and there probably never will be. Make the best of what you have, and utilize every moment you are blessed with.

Make Avon part of your everyday life. My business is a big piece of who I am and it goes with me everywhere. It has become second nature for me. I always carry books and business cards. I wear the jewelry and use the products. My Avon nametag is part of my daily outfit.

Connect. I easily see twenty to thirty people a day just running my routine errands. That means twenty to thirty potential team members or customers. It is up to you to connect with them. It is as easy as opening your mouth and offering a brochure or a business card to everyone you meet.

Manage your time. Be honest with yourself about time management. People often say, "I spent all day on Avon and nothing happened." Did you really spend all day on Avon, or did you lose yourself in Facebook® or an episode of your favorite show?

Keep a journal. Log your normal daily activities in 15-minute increments to see where you actually spend your time. It is eye opening to see how much time you think you work your business versus what you actually do.

Invest in a great calendar system. I use Google® Calendar because I can color code family members, my personal calendar, and my Avon business calendar. When I enter an activity on my computer, it populates on my phone and my tablet, too. It keeps me on task and actually opens up more time to do the things I want to do. Find a calendar that works for you, and stick to it. You can find the time to make your business work.

Sometimes Life Hands You Lemons

In June 2009, I experienced a series of what seemed like panic attacks. I went to the emergency room to get myself checked. A CT scan revealed a lemon-sized brain tumor called a meningioma. I was suddenly not allowed to drive, which was difficult with two school-aged children and a home-based business. I was scheduled to have brain surgery within a month due to the size of the tumor and its location, which threatened my vision, memory and speech.

Fortunately, I had built close relationships with many of my clients who were more than happy to pick up their orders. My family was extremely supportive, drove me where I needed to go, and helped me with brochures and deliveries. I kept in touch with my team via phone and email. Avon representatives I had met online nationwide sent flowers, gift baskets, thoughts and prayers. My children loved hearing the mail truck arrive, and I still have more than 300 cards and letters that people sent me from around the country.

Thankfully, I am cured of the brain tumor and healthy again. Never in a million years would I have called a brain tumor a blessing, but for me, it was. It validated that working for myself was more than a fabulous opportunity. My business could weather any storm and allow me to overcome any obstacle if I did my part.

What Are You Going to Do?

Avon makes me happy. I have been able to spend the best years of my life raising my family. I have met hundreds of great people simply by asking them if they want an Avon brochure. I have developed life-long friendships with Avon ladies around the world. I have helped women earn the money for date nights with their husbands, to pay off debt, to leave a second job, or to go back to school. I have helped some women earn enough money to leave abusive relationships while regaining their sense of confidence and self-esteem. You cannot put a price tag on that.

We all have hard times; the loss of loved ones, job lay-offs or health issues. Avon has been a constant source of income for me without the worry that comes with working for someone else.

We all make the choice to be our own obstacle or our own champion. We have a million excuses for not doing something; therefore, it is imperative to have a million and one reasons why we *can*. If you have the desire to do something great for yourself and for your family, you can succeed. It is up to you to make that choice. What are you going to do?

JENNETT CENNAME PULLEY

Avon® Executive Unit Leader
Honor Society, Avon Team Ambition
804-920-9009
iloveavon@comcast.net
jennett.pulley@gmail.com
www.youravon.com/jpulley
www.start.avon.com Code: JPULLEY

Jennett started with Avon in 2001 with the goal of staying at home with her two beautiful children. Today she is financially independent and has helped countless other women (and a few great men!) achieve their goals and better their lives with Avon.

Over the years, Jennett has earned many awards, including Spirit of Avon and Recruiting Excellence, as well as several trips, including Jamaica, Las Vegas and the Bahamas. Jennett is extremely proud of her team members and credits them for numerous awards they have received in team growth and total unit sales on both the district and divisional level.

Jennett spends her free time with her teenagers, Kaila and Morgan, shopping, doing mud runs, and just being together. In 2014, the three earned their black belts in martial arts and are now working toward their second-degree black belts and becoming certified instructors. Jennett's husband, Scott, is totally outnumbered as the only male in the house and has been putting up with her shenanigans since 1994. She is grateful for his love, support, and encouragement, as well as his endless patience with the Avon boxes that have taken over the garage.

Keep Your Eye on Your Dream

BY SUSAN ROPER

I was born in Vicksburg, Mississippi, and was the youngest of four siblings. I grew up in the Mississippi Delta cotton belt. My dad was a plantation manager and my mom was a stay-at-home mom.

> *"My father taught me always to do more than you get paid for as an investment in your future."*
> **—Jim Rohn, American entrepreneur, author and motivational speaker**

My parents were hard workers, a characteristic my siblings and I definitely inherited from them. I was always very independent, even at age four or five. My father told me that while he was teaching me to ride a bike, I told him I did not need his help. I had to do it all by myself. I guess you can say that I am still that way.

I knew before I graduated high school that I wanted to become a computer programmer. I did not want to waste any time getting started in that field and went to college. I earned my associate degree in data processing in 1978, when computers were far less advanced than they are today. There was no such thing as a personal computer, only mainframe computers. I started out in keypunch in Jackson, Mississippi, and soon landed a job in computer programming in Memphis, Tennessee. Then I was given an opportunity to be a data processing manager for a beverage distributer.

From there I went to work as a systems analyst for a large local bank. I installed computer systems in small banks. I was responsible for installing the hardware, which is the computer system itself, and converting their files of information for the new system. I also worked my way up to manager of the department. After six years, the bank got out of the installing of in-house computer systems. After handling contract-programming jobs for a year, I returned to work for the same bank as a programmer analyst.

My favorite pastime was playing softball. While playing for a co-ed team one fall, I met the man I married three years later.

My precious Katelyn was born on July 4, 1994. When she was six weeks old, I returned to work at the bank and had to put her in daycare. My position at the bank was about to change and it meant working longer hours. That was the last thing I wanted with a newborn at home. I decided to quit my job and use my savings to help pay the bills so that I could stay home with my daughter.

My Why is Katelyn

It is amazing how fast your savings can dwindle. After one year, I had to find something else to do to help with the bills. One day, someone threw an Avon® brochure in my driveway. Even though I had never purchased Avon before, I thought it sounded like something I would like to try. I could stay home, and I would not have to do parties to make sales. Let me tell you that I had never sold anything in my life! However, I knew my friends and family would buy from me.

I called a number in the paper and the district manager came to my house and signed me up. It was February 1996, when managers could sign up recruits for leadership representatives.

I went to my first sales meeting a few weeks after signing up and soon found out about Avon's leadership program. Our manager always shared what her representatives were earning in the program in her district. When I saw what my upline was earning, I knew that the leadership program would be the way for me to earn the full-time salary I needed.

Training for leadership was limited back then; however, my district manager was great in teaching us how to help representatives. I will never forget the first time she took me out to show me how to do an appointment. I was so excited! I was on my way to building my team and my future.

On My Way to Success

It took me two and a half months to make the first level in the leadership program. There were no bonuses to be made back then, and my first check was $12. Wow, that was a lot of time and effort for $12! Yet I did not mind because I knew that if I stayed focused on my goal of making it to the top earning level in leadership, I would see the big money. Success never happens overnight and nothing worth having is really easy to obtain.

I also realized that to be successful, you need to read and study everything you can about your business. I purchased all types of books and audios on network marketing. I loved to listen to Jim Rohn when I needed a boost in motivation.

> *"Resolve to pay any price or make any sacrifice to get into the top ten percent of your field. The payoff is incredible!"*
> —**Brian Tracy, Canadian entrepreneur, public speaker, author and personal and professional development trainer**

My Life Changed

My daughter was three when my husband decided to leave our marriage. Now I really had to make a full-time income. I still did not want to put my daughter in daycare and have someone else raise her. I opened a daycare of my own in my home. That way Katelyn would be with me and I could continue to grow my Avon business part time. I cared for her and five other children from 7:00 a.m. to 6:00 p.m., Monday through Friday. Most of them came to me as newborns.

Each day, after my daycare closed, and on the weekends, I would do Avon appointments and deliveries with my daughter by my side. She was only three and four during that time. My family thought I had lost my mind! My father constantly asked when I was going to go out and get a real job. Yet I knew if I stayed focused, I could achieve the dream of earning enough through my Avon business to support my daughter and me.

> *"Obstacles are what you see when you take your eyes off your goals."*
> —**Brian Tracy, Canadian entrepreneur, public speaker, author and personal and professional development trainer**

When I talk to other representatives about my journey, I tell them to imagine you have blinders that prevent you from looking to either side of you. You can only see what is in front of you to stay focused on what it is you want to achieve. It is so easy to get discouraged when you begin to listen to others' negative thoughts. It is so much easier to give in and give up and say *I can't* than to stay on course and say *I can, and I will never give up.*

> *"Resolve in advance to persist until you succeed,*
> *no matter what the difficulty."*
> **—Brian Tracy, Canadian entrepreneur, public speaker, author**
> **and personal and professional development trainer**

Business Improves

I did everything I could to find recruits. I nailed signs on posts, delivered countless brochures in neighborhoods, and ran ads in papers. I tried everything I read about or learned about in sales meetings.

You have to do it more than once to see results. The downfall of many is that they do not see results from doing something just once, so they never try again.

I made it to the next level in Avon's leadership program, Advance Unit Leader (AUL), in 1999 and to the subsequent level, Executive Unit Leader (EUL), in 2000. With each new level, my checks doubled.

I was able to close my daycare when my daughter was almost five and become a full-time Avon representative. When she started kindergarten, I had more time available to really build my downline. Every night, I would schedule the next day so that I could take advantage of every minute I had while Katelyn was in school.

In 2001, I made it to the top level in Avon's leadership program, Senior Executive Unit Leader (SEUL). It took me a lot longer than most to make it to the top level, yet I did not let that discourage me. I persevered and knew that if I kept doing what I was already doing I would get there, and my checks would continue to grow.

"Leaders grow; they are not made."
—Peter Drucker, Austrian-born American management consultant, educator and author

Avon had an incentive in 2010 in which we could double our income for five campaigns. I achieved it for all five. Where could you do that working for someone else? I was able to buy my daughter her first car and a new Apple® computer.

Avon has given me the opportunity to go on trips to places I would never have been able to go on my own, working for someone else. I have earned several Bahaman cruises, several Alaskan cruises, trips to Hawaii, Puerto Rico and lots of others. I have also earned 19 Mrs. Albee awards—one for each year I have been with Avon.

In 2012, I earned a trip to Jamaica that was scheduled for January of 2013. Unfortunately, I could not attend because I had a sudden illness. I was hospitalized for three weeks after major surgery on Christmas Day 2012. I also had another major surgery three months later, which kept me from attending the second trip, to Hawaii, in 2012. The best thing about network marketing is that you earn residual income. The fact that I was in the hospital and then needed time off to recover for six months did not change the amount I was earning. My checks were still being deposited every two weeks by Avon.

Change the Direction of Your Sail

It is hard for some to imagine that they can achieve the highest level in network marketing in any company. Many start to try and then they give up when the first storm blows in and sets their sails in the wrong direction. As a result, they stay where they are and never try for it again. Some begin a new business, and when they don't see themselves moving ahead fast enough or they lose members of their team, they decide it is no longer worth trying, and they give up.

I have been there too. However, when I wanted to quit, I realized that some will and some will not. So what? Who's next? If I have days when I feel defeated, I always remember my favorite Bible passage: "I can do all things through Christ who strengthens me." —Philippians 4:13. I listen to my Jim Rohn audio and my motivation is back.

> *"Giant oaks do grow from little acorns;*
> *but first you must have an acorn!"*
> **—Denis Waitley, American motivational speaker and writer,**
> **consultant and best-selling author**

Everyone Has to Start with One

We all had to start with one team member. The reason we made it all the way to the top is that we never gave up. We only stopped what was not working and looked for other ways to make it work. What works for some leaders does not work for others. You have to find what works for you in your business and always be willing to try to improve on it. Successful leaders never stop trying to learn new ways to improve their business. That is why we still attend seminars and meetings, and we read new books about our business.

I teach my team members that they have not met their "gold nugget recruit" yet, and that is why they must prospect daily. It may be the bank teller, the nurse at your doctor's visit, the salesperson in your favorite store, the lady sitting next to you at the nail salon, or the receptionist at the insurance office. Offer your opportunity to everyone you meet. You never know when you are going to strike gold. Try to talk to at least three or four people a day while you are out running your errands.

Be prepared with extra brochures. They can start taking orders right away, and you can schedule an appointment with them to officially sign them up.

If someone is a no-show to their appointment, then look for someone else while you are there. You can do this by displaying a sign saying "Help Wanted" or "Free Samples" where you are sitting. In other words, have a backup plan so you do not go home empty handed.

Other ways to help build your business:
- Always wear a name badge or something advertising your business.
- Advertise with a magnetic sign or window sticker on your vehicle.
- Put a sign in your yard, if your city allows it.
- Look for directory listings that allow you to list your business.
- Post on Twitter®, Facebook® and LinkedIn®.
- Always have business cards to hand out.
- Look for bulletin boards to post a sign or business cards.

Babe Ruth hit 714 home runs, but he struck out 1,330 times in his career. He said, "Every strike brings me closer to the next home run." R.H. Macy failed seven times before his store in New York City caught on. Henry Ford failed and went broke five times before he succeeded. Vince Lombardi wrote, "It's not whether you get knocked down; it's whether you get back up." Your success will not happen overnight. Give yourself time to build your business. Focus on where you want to be in your business and then do not stop until you make it happen!

SUSAN ROPER

Avon® Senior Executive Unit Leader
Rose Circle
Susan's Super Stars Team
901-270-0296
srop1007@bellsouth.net
www.youravon.com/sroper
www.startavon.com, ref code: sroper

Susan was born in Vicksburg, Mississippi. She currently lives in Bartlett, Tennessee, and has one daughter. She graduated from MDJC with an associate degree in data processing.

Susan has been with Avon since 1996. She runs a growing Avon business of nearly $3 million with the help of her team. Susan was named Best New Performer for her district the first year in her business. She has achieved numerous recruiting awards and trips. In 2001 and 2011, Susan received the prestigious Spirit of Avon Award in her district. In 2012, she earned the Recruiting Excellence Award. She has been at the top level of Senior Executive Unit Leader with Avon since 2001.

Susan's key to success is perseverance. She teaches to never, never, never give up, and you will achieve your dreams and goals. Focus on where you want to be, and do not let distractions get in your way.

Keep Going

BY THERESA KRAAI

I was born in Tampa, Florida, as the youngest and only girl out of six children. After my parents separated, my mom moved us to San Francisco, California. As a single mother, she did everything she could do to provide for us. My mom modeled hard work, perseverance, faith, and the values of character.

When I graduated from high school, I thought I was in love and moved to Reno, Nevada, with my boyfriend, where I ended up broke and broken hearted. I took on a job as a cocktail waitress at the Peppermill Hotel and Casino.

After a year and a half, I lost my cocktail waitress job due to tendonitis, so I worked part time as a real estate office receptionist and part time at Subway® sandwiches. However, I could not earn as much money as I had at the casino.

In December 1989, I answered an ad in the newspaper about Avon®. A little ol' lady came over, signed me up, accepted my appointment fee, and left without ever following up.

My neighbor, who had sold Avon before, suggested that I order lipstick and perfume samples. She recommended I check the jewelry and makeup to make sure it was not damaged and this taught me about the product. I purchased a pink tackle box, filled it with samples, order forms and Avon books, and took them to the casino to sell to my cocktail waitress friends.

Shortly thereafter, life fell apart, and I moved back to San Francisco. I worked with my mother as a food server in an upscale retirement home and began selling Avon products to my co-workers.

Each year, at the close of our fiscal cycle, I would make "midnight President's Club calls"—calling each customer from my receipts and asking if they would buy their favorite perfume, mascara, bubble bath, or lipstick, and letting them know if it was on sale. I kept calling customers until I reached my goal, even if it took me all night. One year, I literally made President's Club (PC) with a surplus of $5—talk about by the skin of my teeth!

Choosing Leadership

Without an upline or a district sales manager (DSM) to connect with, I was content with simply selling enough for PC each year. In the third year of my Avon business, my area got a new divisional manager. She and my DSM reached out to me to get me started in the leadership program. I signed up one person.

In 1993, I met my husband-to-be and we married in 1995. I was finishing up my associate's degree and selling Avon to my classmates and teachers while working full time at the retirement home. In 1999, we were blessed with a little girl and began house hunting. San Francisco was unaffordable, so we chose to live in a little city I had never heard of: Pittsburg, California.

I knew no one in Pittsburg to sell Avon to, however; so I used the Power of 3. I talked to everybody I came in contact with about Avon, and I quickly grew a new customer base. Moving there blessed me with an incredible DSM who encouraged me to join leadership again. This time I took it a little more seriously—just a little.

After six months and one day, I recruited my fifth person. I was a day too late and exceeded Avon's time limit to reach Unit Leader! I lost my first four recruits and was back to the drawing board with just one team member. I felt dejected and incompetent. I felt like a fool, an idiot, and a failure. I realize these are harsh words, but that was the negative self-talk I carried with me. Pursuing leadership lost its thrill. I was convinced that the only profitable path was through sales.

In 2002 I had my second child, became my mother's full-time caregiver, and made Rose Circle by selling $38,000 worth of product. How? By taking books with me to every doctor appointment and errand, and being sure to collect contact information to follow up.

Don't Listen to the Naysayers

I was not surrounded by cheerleaders. My own husband told me I was good at sales and should stick with that. Another person said, "No one can really make money at Avon," implying Avon is a racket. My financial advisor said, "Oh, people can make money in Avon. I just don't know if *you* can."

Then my incredible DSM left Avon, and the new one would introduce me by saying, "This is Theresa Kraai, 19 years with Avon, career Unit Leader." She constantly reminded me of how much money I was leaving on the table. That was not very motivating.

I trudged along and occasionally added a new team member. I almost titled Advanced Unit Leader (AUL) twice before I actually made it in 2011. My team was not strong because when I signed someone up I would say, "Oh, you don't have to do leadership; that's optional." I had my team convinced that participating in leadership was a betrayal to sales!

I got another new DSM in 2011 who worked relentlessly to change my thinking. Still, I continued to struggle with motivation. I came up with all kinds of excuses about why I was not advancing: I had three children under the age of eight, it was difficult to find good people, I was my mother's caregiver, I had no car, my husband worked twelve hours, it was too hot, too cold, I had PMS. All these excuses led to more guilt—and guilt is not a motivator!

Discovering My Why

Then, someone told me I needed to find my why. I came up with some socially acceptable *whys:* get my family out of debt, pay for kids' college, and save for retirement. However, none of these reasons to succeed truly moved me. While they were good reasons, they were not my reasons; they were what society said I should want. I had a major disconnect, and it was keeping me stumped. I could not figure it out.

A wise friend encouraged me to do one thing every day to move my business forward, whether it was labeling books, preparing sign-up kits, dropping books on doorsteps and in parking lots, or sending emails. This would ensure I would have done one thing each day, and on Friday I could feel good about myself instead of feeling incompetent. I kept going.

I discovered that my disconnect came from my negative self-talk. I wondered why I was so harsh with myself. It turns out that skeletons in the closet do not die. When I was three years old, one of my brothers began abusing me. As I grew into adulthood, false shame and fear haunted me. Through counseling, and by God's grace, I was able to get out from underneath all those lies that were holding me back and begin to move forward.

Persevering Through Fear

Without acknowledging the root cause of my emotions, I felt as though I was in a black hole. The hardest emotion to get through was fear. In the summer of 2013, I hired a business coach who helped me to see that I was afraid of success! I believed people would not like me anymore. Some people offer a shoulder to cry on when you do not make it, yet do not support you in your success. I was terrified of that rejection; so much so, that I sabotaged my own efforts by trying to make sure that everyone liked me.

I am grateful that Avon does not fire us for not performing right away! I was able to make money while I went through life's ups and downs and while I sorted myself out. When I did not want to see or talk to anyone, I could still work my business in ways that I was comfortable with: emails, texts, Facebook® and book drops. Even when the only thing that got me out of bed was that I had to get the kids to school, I could still make money with Avon. If I had a traditional job, I am sure I would have been written up and fired!

Knowing what my fear was, I could now face it head-on. When my stomach tightened, when I felt panicked, when I wanted to hide in my house and clean, I knew it was because I was on the verge of a success—title advancements in my team or increasing sales—and I could choose to keep going. It's funny how the good things that happen can either immobilize or energize us, depending on how we choose to look at them.

A few months later, I heard that "Your *why* should make you cry." My socially acceptable *whys* did not make me cry. I tried adding a horse, a motorcycle, and a Mercedes® to my dream board, but I still did not cry. Did I not want anything?

I struggled with the notion of being rich. I did not want to become money-hungry or be consumed by materialism. What *did* I want? What was my *why?* I had to close my eyes and plug my ears to block out everybody and their notions of what was best for me to get down to the real-me *why*. After several efforts to get to this layer, I finally found my *why!* When I spoke the words to myself, I could barely squeak it out in a whisper. I get teary-eyed just thinking about it!

Before I share my *why,* I ask that you not laugh at or judge me without hearing me out. My *why* is because I want to shop with cash. (My hands are shaking while I type this.) I grew up dirt poor. No, I did not walk to and from school, in the snow and uphill both ways—it does not snow in San Francisco, though we do have plenty of hills! My mom, God bless her soul, raised six kids on her own, and things were scarce.

My parents divorced when I was three. Although my dad visited, the financial burden was all on my mom. She was the manager of our apartment building so that we could have cheap rent for our two-bedroom apartment. When it rained, Mom would cut holes out of the bottoms of garbage bags and pull them over our heads to use as ponchos as we walked downtown to get our welfare checks and food stamps. People showed up with groceries because God put it in their hearts to do so. Our Christmas toys came from the fire department. My clothes came from the Purple Heart Thrift Store or were hand-me-downs from my dad's girlfriend's daughters. (That was weird, but the clothes were nice, so I used them). My mom put so much white shoe polish on my sneakers to keep them white that they bubbled in the rain! Yep, we were poor.

After five boys, my mom had me when she was 44. We were best buddies. My mom worked very hard to provide for us. She gave us all she could. There was a lot we could not participate in. One of my mom's greatest joys was to buy me a new outfit. She would forfeit getting a top for herself or getting her hair done because she wanted to get me something cute to wear.

I could see a sadness in my mom's eyes. She grew up during the Depression and has incredible stories of perseverance. She lived in camps with her paraplegic mother and little brother. She would search trashcans for mustard greens, wash them off, and feed them to her brother. She wanted to give her kids what she could never have growing up. Mom and I enjoyed simple pleasures like shopping and having hot buttered popcorn and classic Coke® while watching a good 49ers game.

When I finally reached Senior Executive Unit Leader in 2014, I realized my goal of shopping with cash at Nordstrom®. A part of me said, "Look, Mom, I made it! No more Purple Heart!" My successes with Avon enabled me to accomplish what my mom always longed to do, but never could: to lavish on her family the finer things in life. My mom passed in 2006, and in a weird, subconscious way, being able to shop with cash was a tribute to my mother, who instilled in us the value of hard work. She taught us to never give up and just *keep going*. I love you, Mom!

Not everyone is going to understand my *why*, and that's okay. It is not their *why*, it is mine. That is what I want my team members to understand. When I realized my *why*, it was as though someone was holding a gorgeous, new wardrobe in front of me and not letting me have it. I could feel those soft fabrics on my skin. I could see myself not tugging on my clothes, trying to make them fit right. I could see myself walking into a room with confidence.

Success Despite Setbacks

My *why* is so powerful that it sustained me while going from AUL to EUL. Then, with just two more ULs needed to get to SEUL, I lost two instead and went back to AUL. I missed the trip to Jamaica by one order. I missed the $5000 bonus. I even missed winning a beach towel. I told my DSM, "I don't want to play anymore! I can't even win a beach towel!" I pouted for two weeks and then picked myself back up. I am a waitress by trade. Do you know how many hours I would have to work to earn the kind of income I can in Avon? I would be crippled and still would not come close. Vondell McKenzie started her Avon business when she was 65, and today she is one of the top leaders in Avon. I do not care how long this takes; I am going to keep going all the way to the top!

In Campaign 7 2014, I advanced to Senior Executive Unit Leader. There are no words to explain how thrilled, amazed, and astonished I am! This year has been unbelievable. I was number two in the Nation for the Grow to Go to Mexico incentive trip and valedictorian of the AUL Academy. And my team, The Dazzling Diamonds, ranked number seven in the Nation for Total Unit Sales Increase.

The Dazzling Diamonds is an amazing team. It is an honor and a privilege to be involved in the lives and dreams of my team members. I am truly blessed. If I have a team member complain about being a Unit Leader for what they perceive is too long, I remind them of my story and tell them the income is well worth the journey—just *keep going!*

Life has seasons of ups and downs. As Avon representatives, we are blessed to be able to customize our businesses. There were times when I could not give my business 100 percent of my attention. Through consistent practices though, I could keep my business going. By continuously planting seeds, training and motivating my team, we were able to achieve national recognition. I encourage you to keep going, whether you have been working your business for one year or twenty years. The rewards and personal growth are well worth it!

THERESA KRAAI

Avon® Senior Executive Unit Leader
Dazzling Diamonds

855-qwn-avon
theresak@avonca.us
www.youravon.com/tkraai

Theresa has been with Avon since 1989. She first tried leadership in 1993, and became a Unit Leader in 2001. Ten years later, Theresa advanced to Advanced Unit Leader. Her business grew in 2011, during which she advanced title three times and achieved a team sales increase of more than $250,000 per year over a period of four years.

In 2014, Theresa earned a Senior Executive Unit Leader title, completed the AUL Academy as valedictorian, reached the #2 rank in the Grow to Go to Mexico leadership incentive, and earned the #7 national award for total unit sales increase. Plus, her total unit sales volume exceeded $1 million for the first time.

Theresa was born in Florida and raised in San Francisco by her single mother. Theresa lives in the Bay Area with her husband, three children and six pets. She is involved in her church and enjoys meeting new people, fancy coffee drinks, trips to new places, dancing with her husband, and anything that goes fast. She looks forward to using the fruits of her success to help others, give nice gifts, and buy things that go fast.

Face Your Fears and Reach Success

BY LISA MONOSON

I silently struggled with an affliction for most of my life: anxiety and panic disorder. I believed that disclosing my fears to others would be embarrassing and a sign of weakness. However, although my story is personal, I hope it will inspire you and give you hope to overcome your own trials and tribulations.

I was raised in beautiful Palm Beach, South Florida. My father was a hardworking man with a heart of gold. My mother was a caring, stay-at-home mom who raised my younger brother and me.

With a strong faith and supportive parents, I was a fortunate girl who had what any kid needed. Sundays were always special. Every week after church we would gather together with family and enjoy a huge Italian feast.

I attended Catholic school and was a typical kid who was not overly popular. I was always there for a friend in need. Many kids ostracized me for not being rich. The lack of materialistic possessions did not bother me because I had something much greater: a huge, loving family.

When I was 13 years old I started a new public school. The stress of change, middle school and peers caused me terrible anxiety, which spiraled into physical illness. This led to the vicious cycle of panic and anxiety attacks.

I learned in middle and high school that kids can be mean-spirited. I believed no one had the right to tear you down. Each of us was wonderfully and beautifully made, and *everyone* had a gift to give. I wore my heart on my sleeve and even befriended those who were shunned. I realized that it was your inside confidence that really mattered—not popularity, beauty or what others thought of you. What *you* think of *you* matters.

A New Beginning

Even before adulthood, I had an entrepreneurial spirit. I was a Girl Scout and participated in community service. To make extra money, I would craft and sell items such as hair accessories. I babysat and sold fruit from our backyard tree, door to door. When school had fundraisers, I strived to sell the most in order to get the prizes and help the class win the pizza party.

I dreamed of being a mom, marrying a wonderful husband, and becoming a nurse, actress, model or cosmetologist. At age 17, I met Robert. We had a storybook romance. We were young and in love when he joined the Marines and left for war. After exchanging hundreds of letters, he returned to a tearful, joyous reunion. We got married in 1992.

Before our first child, Kyle, was born, I began working at a church pre-school across the street from our apartment; working close to home helped with my anxiety. After maternity leave, I returned to work at the daycare and brought my son with me. When he was a year old, I stayed home with him full time and opened my own home day-care business.

When our second son, Zach, was born, we built our first house. Running the daycare and being my own boss gave me the control I needed with my anxiety issues.

My third pregnancy made me ill, and I had to close the daycare. However, we still needed the extra income and I had to make money from home to be with my children.

At a local playgroup that I belonged to, one of the moms started selling Avon®. I inquired, "What do you have to do to sell Avon?" She told me starting up was inexpensive and all she had to do was share the book with others, take and place orders, and earn money. It all sounded too good to be true. I signed up and my Avon journey began. I was eager to learn and asked a lot of questions. I began absorbing as much information as I could from the kit that was given to me and online. I took brochures with me everywhere and sent them with neighbors to work.

By the time my son Jacob was born three months later, I had started a team of several clients interested in selling. Sharing Avon became natural and part of my daily routine. Team growth and development was inevitable.

In my first cycle with Avon, I made President's Club. I loved con-necting with people, being a mom, and the ability to handle my anxiety issues without pressure from a boss.

A new challenge came in 2002. When our middle child, Zach, was four, he was dismissed from preschool. We had him tested and learned that he has Asperger's Syndrome, a form of autism. Thanks to my Avon business, I was available to help my son when he needed me most.

After years of trying different medications, my anxiety episodes worsened in 2006-2008. I had made Advanced Unit Leader (AUL), and we had just moved to a new home. I was across town from where we lived before and decided not to keep clients that far away due to my anxiety. I had to start over in our new area. When my youngest son was at school and Robert was at work, I was all alone in a big new house and knew no one. I started having severe panic attacks.

When I drove, I often turned the car around and went right back home. Sometimes I would leave carts of groceries in the store to bolt home, shaking and terrified. I wondered how I could be a good mother and businesswoman when my health was out of control.

The panic and anxiety attacks caused physical illness. Eventually I did not want to leave my home. It was so bad that I became agoraphobic, perceiving places outside my home as dangerous or uncomfortable. I was trapped inside my home, drowning by my fears and anxiety. As I lay in my bed one day, I wondered how it got to that point. Fearful, I contemplated ending my life. I felt like a burden to my family. Anxiety and panic led to deep depression.

Each day, I woke up feeling sick to my stomach, shedding many tears and fearing how I would face the day. It seemed I had no way out. I was shameful of letting my kids see me like that. I prayed for God to heal me. I constantly thought of my family and how selfish it would be to put my children through losing me. That kept me going.

My Avon business was there for me even in that dark time, still providing for us even though I was not at my best. Clients picked up orders from my house or my superman of a husband delivered, and I never missed an order. I had an Avon helper generating sales for me. A nurse came to my home because I could not go to a doctor's office. I felt worthless.

After many medication changes, along with prayer and therapy, the right combination started to work. I began venturing out again on short trips and regained some control.

Kicking Anxiety to the Curb

"Struggling and suffering are the essence of a life worth living.
If you're not pushing yourself beyond the comfort zone…
You're denying yourself an extraordinary trip."
—Dean Karnazes, American ultramarathon runner and author

To get through each day, I made sure not to overschedule myself. Venturing out again each day, I would do a little more, taking baby steps, and knowing I was in control and could leave if necessary.

Working my business was a great distraction from my fears. I would set goals for when I was out and use the "power of three," sharing the brochures and opportunity with at least three people each day. Avon was good therapy for me and kept my mind busy enough to avoid going into full-blown panic attacks. Little by little, I was improving and becoming the mom I once was. I felt I had purpose, and my business was thriving again.

"Life isn't about waiting for the storm to pass;
it's about learning to dance in the rain…"
—Vivian Green, American singer, songwriter and pianist

In my early years as a leader, I held bi-monthly conference calls. Then in 2009, I started a team website to give my team additional support. I also created a YouTube™ channel to train, inspire and mentor my team. It was an ingenious way for me to connect and teach others, even those out of state, without physically leaving home. Videos were only a click away at the convenience of representatives.

I realized that automation would greatly help my business. I had been repeating the same information in emails and phone trainings and discovered that videos provided an additional resource for distributing information. I created more videos, ranging from representative training, to beauty tutorials, to product reviews.

My videos and team website are now open to help any Avon representative. People from all over the world express how the videos and connections have helped their teams and districts. I believe God continues to bless me for sharing my passion with others.

I have grown on social media platforms, and new representatives have joined my team as a result of my exposure through YouTube, blogging, Pinterest®, Facebook® and Twitter®. I hold virtual meetings for my team and adoptees from all over the world. Representatives from other countries have contacted me, joined our team site, watched my videos, and followed me on social media. Start taking advantage of technology in your business and you can touch the world.

Breaking through Barriers

In 2009, I created a plan to get to Executive Unit Leader (EUL) by December. I contacted leads from my home and scheduled several appointments per week in my home office when my husband was at home. I held team meetings at my community clubhouse or at my home. I made things work for me despite my health issues, thanks to the flexibility of my Avon business.

After being an AUL for too long, I advanced to EUL and was strong. I have advanced slowly, yet my business foundation will be solid when I advance to Senior Executive Unit Leader (SEUL).

Ask, or the Answer Is Always No

Prospecting for customers and recruits is part of your daily activities. Let your business run through you with passion and excitement. You are the boss! Be consistent in your activities to reap the biggest reward.

Do not just wait for things to happen. As a business owner you must make things happen by planning. Schedule time for doing the tasks you may not like doing, such as stamping books, filing paperwork or making calls. My children went with me to all the places I prospected. They helped me stamp and label books and hang them on doors. You can make your business a fun family project. Do not let having children stop you from working your business—they are probably the reason you have it to begin with. Prospects will respect that you involve your kids and see that if you can do it, so can they.

You Can Make Excuses or Money, Not Both

When starting a business, many people fear that they will not have customers, or that they will not know how to recruit. Those are skills you learn with practice. Here are some tips on how to effectively approach prospects:

• Hand people brochures like gifts and say *this is for you*. People do not turn away from a free gift.

- Plant a verbal seed. Share that you are looking for people in the area who need to earn additional income. *Oh, by the way, we are looking for people…*
- Ask for leads. *If you know anyone, please send them my way?*
- Explain the benefits. *It's only $15 to get started.*
- Hand people your card to plant a subliminal seed in a non-confrontational way.
- Ask for their phone numbers to contact them about order dates, special offers, extra samples and product information.

If you share the savings, you will get the sales. Point out special offers. Give personalized service—if you know a client loves butterflies, draw attention to the page with new butterfly jewelry. When you provide caring service, people appreciate it and are more likely to make a purchase.

Imagine, Dream, Inspire

Although panic and anxiety still creep up, nothing can stop me now. Flying and travel, for example, were things I could hardly dream of; however, when I earned *three* trips with Avon in 2013, I spent months preparing myself to face my fears and fly. I knew it was God saying, "It's time, Lisa. Don't worry. I will be with you." I had to prove to myself I could get through it. I knew the journey would provide positive experiences I would never forget.

While building my business, I want to help as many people as I can along the way to achieve their dreams and goals. We use heart-centered, "all about you" coaching with our team, the *Team Money Makers.* Focus on your team, your vision and your plan.

Never Give Up

Life's challenges can make you stronger and help you overcome obstacles. Who you are is the summation of every decision you have made up to this point in your life. Will you choose to be amazing or to be mediocre?

Avon has been a blessing to me and my family. I have been blessed to touch so many lives in my business. I am proud to be an Avon lady and a national leader with 400+ team members.

There will be tears of struggle and tears of joy on your journey. Brush yourself off and persevere, even if the timing is not what you had hoped. Remove the word *quit* from your vocabulary. Travel your journey at your own pace. If you are dedicated, passionate, and prepared to accept the peaks and valleys, you will be successful. When life has its struggles, always remember to "Just keep swimming!"

LISA MONOSON

Avon® Executive Unit Leader

855-5-SellAvon/855-573-5528
lisa@teammoneymakers.com
www.lisamonoson.com
www.yourbeautylady.com
www.youtube.com/lisamonoson

Lisa's entrepreneurial spirit has been a part of her from a young age. She is a wife, a mother to three sons, and resides in Jacksonville, Florida. Joining Avon in 2000, Lisa never expected it would become a full-time career. Living with anxiety and panic disorder, a son with Asperger's, and other health conditions, Lisa has proven that you can conquer, adapt and overcome.

Lisa achieved PC-Rose Circle in sales, Beauty Advisor, Anew® Skincare specialist, and was honored to receive the Spirit of Avon Award in 2009. She has an office full of trophies for her Team Money Makers being in the top three in her district and division. Lisa earned the title of Southeast Regional Makeup Maven in 2013. She is Elite Certified with DSWA and was featured in Avon Maven Videos, *Representative Times*, *What's New*, and *Avon Insider*. In 2014, she made the cover of both Distributor Magazines: *Careers* and *Disabled*.

Connect with Lisa @ Facebook.com/lisaavonmonoson. Lisa's team site Teamoneymakers.com has also inspired many representatives all over the world. Lisa and her husband, Robert, are excited about what is ahead for the future as they reach for the company's highest title, that of National Senior Executives.

A Life of Beauty and Strength

Becoming a Steel Butterfly

BY JULIE LEE HOFFMAN

Although I had the normal ups and downs of any kid, I was born with some natural talents that helped me stay on the right path. I thrive on overcoming challenges and doing the "impossible." I enjoy leading for a common cause. I have a strong entrepreneurial heart and an unwavering optimistic spirit.

Throughout my school years, we moved around often. I hated school and often fought with my mom. I skipped school a lot in high school, and I had terrible grades. Still, there were some highlights in my early school years.

In kindergarten, I was wishing upon stars and teaching all of my friends how to do the same. In third grade, I started a friendship bracelet business on the school bus and learned about supply and demand. In fifth grade, I rallied my classmates to boycott school lunches because they were serving us spoiled fruit. That successful campaign got me in trouble! In middle school, I joined an after school club called Youth to Youth, in which I was one of the most successful fundraisers.

Finding My First Passion

When I was entering high school, we were learning about career choices, and I had no idea what I was going to do. When I realized people could get paid to dance, I decided that was what I would do. I was 14 years old, not quite five feet tall, a little overweight, and I had no dance experience. Everyone thought I was crazy and told me I could not do it—except for one teacher who believed in me and pushed me hard. She taught me what the word work meant.

Within three years, I was invited to train at the Bolshoi Ballet in Moscow, Russia, for ten days, over winter break. On the way back home, I negotiated for a full scholarship to train in Philadelphia with the Russian teacher who had taken us. To my good fortune, there was a snowstorm on the way back that delayed our flight, and I called my mom from New Jersey. She did not know about the scholarship until I called her, and I let her know I was going. I asked her to let me come home to get my things and say goodbye, for I had already spoken to the airline about changing my ticket and flying straight to Philadelphia. Although I did not really give her a choice, my mom agreed and I went to get my things. I dropped out of high school and moved to Philadelphia to live with my new teacher and train.

My persistence and determination paid off. By the age of twenty, I received my first professional contract to join the Colorado Ballet in Denver. From there I joined USA Ballet in Illinois, and met a boy. I fell in love very quickly and married young. A year later, we had a little girl named Sylvia, and I entered back into the ballet world.

Peoria Ballet was my next stop. I danced in a variety of wonderful roles until the company unexpectedly folded. Determined not to go back home to New York, we moved to Atlanta, Georgia, where The Georgia Ballet welcomed me into its company with open arms.

Life in the ballet world was fantastic. However, things were not good at home, and my husband and I divorced when Sylvia was only in preschool. I became a single mom with very few financial resources and no family nearby.

The End of a Career

Then in 2009 my life really fell apart. I had unknowingly broken a small floating bone in my foot and the injury ended my career prematurely. I did not know what to do next. I realized I had started wanting more from life even before my career ended. I had been living the life of a "starving artist" for years and did not want that to be my life forever. I did not want to raise my young daughter, Sylvia, in poverty.

Sylvia needed me to be available for her when she was in school. She was accelerating academically, yet behind socially. I would often have to pick her up from school in the middle of the day for behavioral issues. Later I would come to learn that she was showing the signs of Asperger's, which is a high-functioning form of autism.

When I read books about wealth and prosperity while I was still a dancer, I learned about incredible things people were able to do financially. I was totally fascinated with what was possible and had decided to become a millionaire when my dance life ended. To gain freedom and give my daughter a life of prosperity, I needed to do something differently.

Going Full Speed in a New Direction

Not knowing what to do to make money, I tried cosmetology school and found that I had some natural talent. I continued to read everything I could about wealth building and learned that a network marketing business could be the path to reach my lofty financial goals. While I was dancing and traveling, Avon® had come in and out of my life. I often dabbled with it as a representative myself, yet never did more with it. However, reading about network marketing led me to see that it could be the perfect opportunity for me.

In the winter of 2011, while still in cosmetology school, I became determined once again to make something work. I decided to become an Avon business owner with an amazing woman and leader, Pat Puzder. Cosmetology was not working out for me, as I got in trouble often for selling products and meeting my downline during school hours. Soon, I dropped out and got a full-time job at a local dance store as a pointe shoe fitter instead. This helped pay my bills while I built my Avon business as fast as I could.

And I did grow my business fast. I started in campaign 7, made leadership in campaign 8, promoted to Unit Leader in campaign 9, became Advanced Unit Leader in campaign 13, and finished my first cycle at Honor Society level with personal sales of $20,200+. Just over one year after starting my business, I achieved the title of Executive Unit Leader (EUL), which at the time was the second highest level of the pay plan with Avon. Later that year, I was able to quit my job at the dance store. I told everyone that I fired my boss, because quitting sounded like failure, and in fact, I was being liberated!

From Rags to Riches

My Avon business has changed life drastically for Sylvia and me. I remember being so broke that our heat was cut off for months in the winter. To get warm, we would lie together in bed with our Chihuahua. Sylvia believed we only slept that way because we loved each other so much. I felt so humiliated when we had to bathe at a friend's house because we had no hot water. What got me through that period was reading and watching Lisa Wilber's Avon story. She had also been through difficult times and had come out of it living a life full of financial rewards.

While working full time and building my business, other obstacles tried to throw me off my course. A police officer pulled me over for driving without car insurance, which I could not afford. My driver's license was revoked for three months, and I had no permit to drive to work. Part of the sentence also included three months of community service at a local church as a custodian to pay off the $2,000 fine. My parents moved from New York to Georgia to live with me, and we crammed into my apartment until we could find a house to rent. Sylvia's social problems at school escalated and she was suspended frequently, eventually resulting in a year of homeschooling. Obstacles and pressures happen to everyone, and when they do, we must keep pushing through to get to the other side.

Today I continue to live modestly and am nowhere near a millionaire yet; however, life is vastly different from before. I have a new, beautiful car, a Mazda® 3 I call "Jackie." If I want to indulge with a hot bubble bath in the afternoon, I give myself the luxury. Sylvia and I eat well, and we no longer share a bed, because we can adjust the heater to whatever temperature we please. Although the occasional bad dream will bring her to me, I only pretend to mind. She takes

Tae Kwon Do and has new clothes when she hits a growth spurt. Sylvia is a straight-A student, and if she has a little bump in her day, I am available to go to her.

Attaining Personal Growth

Avon has not only changed my life financially, it has grown me as a person. I have the confidence to talk to strangers and attract the type of people I want to become like. I am no longer intimidated by people I admire, because I am comfortable with myself.

Seeing Sylvia thrive shows me I am the mother I want to be. It makes me proud to be able to drive her to school every day and not have to rely on the bus, after-school programs or babysitters. She walks out after school and sees me standing there waiting for her, making her feel safe and giving me great joy.

I am the mentor I want to be. Enhancing women's lives and helping them grow financially and personally fills my heart.

By the time this book goes to print, I will have changed my name from Hayes to Hoffman and married the man of my dreams. It is the new me who was able to attract a man like Karl.

Truly, my prosperity multiplies as I grow along with my business. Continuing to climb to the top, the success I am already enjoying gives me awesome hope for the future. It is exhilarating.

Steps to Success

Reach out to people. My time was extremely limited when I first started building and needed to grow fast. Therefore, my first campaign in business I jumped on an opportunity and set up a table at the largest mall in the southeast of the United States. I was by myself so I recruited new team members who came out to work with me the following days. Below is the system that I used my first year and that worked so well for me:

- Set up a product display with plenty of brochures and samples.
- Include a large vase for a free drawing.
- Provide clipboards with drawing slips that ask three questions: *Do you already have an Avon representative? Would you like to receive brochures on a regular basis? Are you interested in learning how you can earn good money with Avon?*
- Stand in front of your table, offering samples.
- Always speak to everyone within earshot about your Avon business.
- Offer free brochures.
- Encourage people to enter the free drawing.
- Have starter kits available for anyone interested in joining Avon.
- Invite new representatives to join you the following day.

Invest profits back into your business. For my first year, every dime of my earnings went into the business for events and supplies. When my Avon earnings started to match my dance store paycheck, I desperately wanted to quit my full-time job, but Pat told me not to quit yet and keep investing. She encouraged me to keep growing as long as I could stand doing both. It turns out that she was right—it worked!

Learn everything you can. We are not all born with the skills needed to lead a volunteer army one lipstick at a time. However, you can learn the skills. I read, listened and attended everything Pat recommended and more so that I could become a better leader. Becoming a personal growth and leadership nut, I buried myself in anything I could get my hands on.

Discover what makes people tick. Your team grows faster when you learn what makes people tick. Find out what they want. Learn to show them the potential you see in them. Learn to teach them to do for themselves because they want to, and that will make them feel good. People are both simple and complicated. If you understand your team members and potential recruits, then you can help them get what they want in life. This, in return, helps you by threefold.

> *"You can have everything in life you want*
> *if you can just help enough other people get what they want."*
> —**Zig Ziglar, American author, salesman,**
> **and motivational speaker**

What is stopping you now from reaching your full potential? What are you going to push past so that you can have a full and prosperous life? Decide that you are not going to let anything keep you from having the life you deserve. You were born to be prosperous and to fulfill your potential. Become the leader deep within you. Decide what your ideal life would be like, and go there!

JULIE LEE HOFFMAN

Avon® Executive Unit Leader
Honor Society, Makeup Maven
DSWA Elite Leadership Certificate
678-644-7069
uloveavon2@gmail.com
www.lipstickchica.com
www.youravon.com/jh

Born in Rochester, New York, Julie had a successful, professional ballet career that took her around the country. This eventually brought her to Acworth, a suburb of Atlanta, Georgia. After an injury ended her career prematurely, Julie decided to make her new dreams come true with a passion for Avon.

Determined to leave a life of poverty and replace it with prosperity, Julie attacked her Avon business with everything she had. As a single mom working a full-time job at a local dance store, she was still able to become an Executive Unit Leader in just one year.

By the time this book goes to print, Julie Hayes will have married her perfect mate and become Julie Hoffman. She attributes her Avon business with the personal growth that has made her the mother, wife and mentor she is today. Julie hopes that her story has value to offer others and inspires readers to go after the full and abundant life they deserve. To download the drawing slip Julie mentions in her chapter, request to join her open Facebook® group, Astounding Achiever Buddies.

Let Creativity Flow to
Increase Your Income

BY KAREN CRISS

I was born in the early sixties and grew up in the Sand Mountain area of North Alabama. It was a peaceful place a world away from all the turmoil that was going on in Selma and Birmingham.

I was the only child of Randolph and Wanda Bell, who made sure that I had the most perfect childhood a girl could ask for. Dad worked for the Alabama Highway Department and Mom worked part time at my school.

I never felt like an only child. My mom had five siblings who lived within a few miles of us. We attended church functions together at Beulah Baptist Church and had Sunday dinner at the home of my maternal grandparents, Rufus and Florence Lacey, almost every week. My mom and grandmother planted a garden together, and summers were spent canning, freezing and putting up all the homegrown vegetables.

My dad also came from a large family with seven siblings. His folks lived a little farther away, but we got together often at family gatherings. His parents, Mannon and Fannie Bell, were hard-working farmers. I made many great memories with my Bell cousins.

Multi-Level Marketing Shaped My Life

About the time I turned 10 years old, two of my uncles joined Amway®, and my mom and dad soon followed. I had no idea that being exposed to multi-level marketing as a child would have such an impact on my life.

My dad felt that taking summer vacations was important. Sometimes it would just be a quick two-day trip to Six Flags® theme park or to Callaway Gardens® in Georgia. After the family joined Amway, however, those vacations improved significantly.

Every summer during my teenage years, we would travel to the Tom Payne Family Reunion. He was a Triple Diamond Direct Distributor with Amway who organized a trip to an exotic resort for his downline every year. We got chances to stay at the luxurious Fontainebleau Hotel and the Innisbrook Resort, both in Florida, and at Tan-Tar-A in Missouri. These reunions provided me the opportunity to meet Zig Ziglar as well as the top echelon with Amway, such as Dexter Yager and Rick Setzer. I even got the chance to babysit their children while they spoke at the rallies. They would send a limo to pick me up and take me to their hotel to care for their children. This gave me an appetite for the finer things in life, like staying in nice hotels and traveling. At an early age, I was exposed to books about positive thinking, such as *Think and Grow Rich* and *The Magic of Thinking Big*, along with motivational cassettes featuring Amway's famed speakers. These ideas have fashioned my life since that time.

I attended Fyffe Elementary and High School, where football was—and still is—king! I graduated with 82 students, the largest class to graduate from Fyffe up until that time. After graduation, I attended Northeast State Junior College and then relocated to Birmingham to continue my education at the University of Alabama in Birmingham (UAB).

After arriving on campus, I met the love of my life, Larry Criss from Tuscaloosa County, Alabama. We dated throughout college. He graduated with a degree in bio-medical electronic engineering and moved to New Orleans, Louisiana. After I graduated with a degree in mass communications, I set out for New Orleans, where Larry and I were married one week later. We began our life there in 1984. In 1986, he accepted a transfer back to Birmingham with his company. We were thrilled to move back close to friends and family. In 1987, our first child, Lacey, was born, and I became a stay-at-home mom.

The Avon Lady Knocks at My Door

An Avon® lady in my neighborhood would call on me occasionally and I always purchased a little something. She offered me the earning opportunity and submitted my name to the local district manager (DM), Sherri Mauter. I had never heard of anyone who made a living, much less a fortune, as an Avon lady; however, it was only $25 at that time for the kit, and I decided to give it a go. Little did I know how Avon would change my life!

With my baby in tow, I began to build a customer base through territory selling. My family lived a little too far away to get regular orders; therefore, I set about meeting my neighbors. I was encouraged by my DM to attend a local sales meeting. I was amazed at the crowd of friendly, supportive women who attended each month. The DM made the meetings so much fun, filled with surprises, and they were such a great learning experience that it was not uncommon for us to have 75 to 100 representatives in attendance. At these local meetings, I began to see Avon in a very different light.

I made President's Club in my first year of selling. By then, I had fallen in love! Not only with the products and the customers, but also with the many other Avon ladies that I had developed relationships with. I could not imagine my life without them.

At one of these meetings I met Debbie Clemons, a representative. I learned that she was a stay-at-home mom with two daughters and that she earned $1,000 a month. I thought, *if I can make that kind of money, I won't have to go back to work!*

By the time our second daughter, Amy, was born in 1991, I was selling Avon at several businesses referred to me, in addition to my neighborhood. I used the "Mother's Day Out" program at a local church for inexpensive childcare to get my deliveries done. I went on to make Honor Society and then Rose Circle, while increasing my sales and earnings each year. I was earning that $1,000 a month— more than I had dreamed of.

In 1992, with the inception of Avon's leadership program, I began to build the "$ucce$$ Expre$$" Team. In 1994, I earned my first official Avon trip to Las Vegas. There I met many people who were earning over $100,000 a year with their Avon business. I was amazed and could not wait to get back home and do the same. Once again, I was in love with Avon! This company really could change my life as well as the lives of those around me.

In 2001, at age 39, I found out that I was expecting our third daughter, Skylar, and our family was complete!

Trips, Travel and Incentives

Avon has allowed my family to travel to many great locations and to live the lifestyle I had dreamed of as a child. I was fortunate enough in 1999 to be asked to participate in the very first National Convention in Orlando, Florida. I was on the "Rich and Famous" panel, and it was my first taste of an all-expenses-paid trip with Avon. Angie Rossi and Maria Penniger (Sutez) interviewed the panel.

A couple of years later, I also had the honor of being one of the speakers at the Fundraiser Seminar in New Orleans. We had thousands attend the sessions, including then President and CEO of Avon, Andrea Jung. Being an "Avon celebrity" was fun and I loved all the attention!

I earned other trips, including several cruises with the "Anchor's Away" series, which took us to Mexico and the Bahamas. I have also traveled to Las Vegas, Dallas and Orlando. But my favorite trip was to Jamaica. My husband, Larry, was able to go with me and we stayed at a private villa on the beach. It was a luxurious bed and breakfast setting with a bedroom suite all to ourselves. Each morning, we shared breakfast by the villa's private pool, along with other inspirational representatives who had also earned the trip. A maid, a butler, and a chef catered to our every need. My favorite thing was to come home in the evening to find our laundry all washed, pressed, and hanging in the closet, ready to put on for the evening's activities.

Another much-loved trip was the Alaskan Alaskan cruise; after which I was inspired on to Senior Executive Unit Leader. We sailed from Seattle and made stops in Skagway, Juneau, and Victoria, British Columbia. All of my excursions on these trips were paid for by Avon and thanks to President's Points!

In addition to the awesome trips I have earned with Avon, my family and I have been able to go to Disney World® and Universal Studios® in Orlando many times, thanks to my Avon earnings. We have even been able to include our parents on some of these trips.

I have also earned many incentives which have given us new furniture and appliances (through the former Starshares Program). More recently, I received a new IPad®, a 46-inch television, and a Keurig® coffee maker—with free coffee and tea for a year. I encourage you to work on every incentive Avon offers and begin earning all the gifts and trips you can!

We've been able to purchase our home on the lake and spend many afternoons on sunset boat rides, thanks to the flexibility of our Avon business. You can do this too!

Fun and Flexibility

As a result of my Avon career, I have been able to stay at home and raise my three children. My two older daughters now live on their own, and Skylar enters middle school soon. I have never had to miss a school activity, ballgame, theater production or field trip.

The last five years of my dad's life were filled with numerous doctor's visits, surgeries and hospitalizations. I was able to work my Avon career around those crucial appointments. He passed away in October 2014 at the age of 85. I am also able to take care of my mom, who is handicapped, several days each month. If I had a nine-to-five job, I would not have this flexibility.

Sharing the Dream

One of my passions is teaching and training representatives as much as I can about how to sell Avon, build a successful team, and help in their communities with philanthropic efforts. Speaking in front of a small group at my sales meeting is no big deal. After being "thrown" into a crowd of 17,000 screaming Avon representatives at a national convention early in your Avon career, speaking at the sales meeting or local division meeting is a piece of cake!

I regularly hold skin care and fundraiser workshops. We also do many team activities. These include "Fishing on Friday's," "Have a Fantastic Fall!" "Breakfast Bunch," and "Soup, Salad & Success" gatherings. Representatives love having a theme. Use your imagination to come up with a name for everything you do. Feel free to use one of the above ideas, or contact me for more information.

> *"Be an 'activationalist.' Be someone who does things.*
> *Be a doer, not a "don't-er." Use action to cure fear*
> *and gain confidence. Do what you fear,*
> *and fear disappears. Just try it and see."*
> **—David J. Schwartz, American motivational writer, coach**
> **and author of *The Magic of Thinking Big***

Creative Selling with Potty Parties

At one of my early sales meetings, I befriended Jenny Self, a sister representative. She sold exclusively in businesses and took creative selling to the max! When her life took a turn, she could no longer manage her Avon business. She took me under her wing and into her car and took me on the ride of a lifetime to introduce me to her customers. I had never been around anyone who had the knack for sales the way she did. One of Jenny's great sales techniques involved "setting up shop" in the ladies restrooms of local businesses. This works best in a location where you have a connection to give you the "in" you need.

Drop by to show clients the latest goodies from Avon. A wheeled luggage cart—sells for around $19.99—comes in handy to neatly transport your merchandise. Order and price your demos. Also, be sure to scope out the Outlet and the regular brochure for great deals on cash-and-carry items. Customers who never place orders often buy things you have on hand. If the restroom has the space, set up a T.V. tray to display your products. Use a pretty piece of fabric to dress it up a bit. Say something like, "Are you here for the *potty* or the *party?*" to break the ice!

Avon is known for its animated items, especially at holiday time. These cuties must be shown to be sold. Always have batteries installed and you will be amazed at how many orders you can take. If you are in an office of mostly new customers, offer a door-prize drawing to get their contact information for follow up. Often, customers will place their orders on the spot, in addition to purchasing items that you have on hand.

Consider having a demo discount sale each time. Clearly mark each discounted item and explain that the first person to make an offer for the item gets your demo after you show it to all your customers. At some businesses you can do a "Potty Party" each campaign, and at others just once a month or so. The customers begin to look forward to your coming by and it allows you to establish a relationship with them that goes much deeper than when you just drop off brochures. I have taken as much as $1,000 worth of orders during a four-hour stay in a restroom at Christmas time, and you can too!

Tailgate Parties or Trunk Sales

You can turn your automobile into a "sale on wheels." Have your items prepared in the trunk or the back end of your SUV. Be sure to a use pretty cloth to dress it up. Let your customers know that you will be having a tailgate party via a label on your brochure or a flyer in the ladies restroom. Promotion is key! Use many of the ideas from the "Potty Party" for your tailgate party. Customers will often go back into their office and say, "You've just got to come and see what this crazy Avon Lady is doing in the bathroom (or in the parking lot.)" During the holidays, it is not uncommon to make an additional $100 to $200 in profits each campaign by holding sales like this. Do not be afraid to get a little crazy.

> *"Somewhere in your make-up there lies, sleeping,*
> *the seed of achievement which, if aroused*
> *and put into action, would carry you to heights,*
> *such as you may never have hoped to attain!"*
> — **Napoleon Hill, American author of *Think and Grow Rich***

Give It a Go!

With just a little confidence in yourself and your imagination, you will be amazed at what you can do with your Avon business. What sets us apart from retail stores and web-based businesses is that personal touch that only you can offer. Customers love interacting with you and your family and will become much more than clients— they will become your life-long friends.

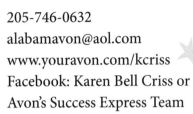

KAREN CRISS
Avon® Executive Unit Leader

205-746-0632
alabamavon@aol.com
www.youravon.com/kcriss
Facebook: Karen Bell Criss or
Avon's Success Express Team

Raised on Sand Mountain in Alabama, Karen Criss was exposed to mulit-level marketing at an early age. The great influences in her life include Zig Ziglar, Jim Rohn, her Dad, Randolph Bell, and many of the top echelon of Amway® Corporation.

After college graduation and marriage, Karen chose to set her career aside and became a stay-at-home mom. She started Avon in 1987 as an avenue to meet her neighbors and make new friends. Karen has sold at Avon's McConnell Club level and achieved Senior Executive Unit Leader. She was featured at the Avon National Representative Conventions in 1999 and 2001 as a speaker on the Rich and Famous Panel and the Fundraiser Seminars. Karen has earned many trips and cruises with Avon, with destinations that included Jamaica, the Bahamas and Alaska, to name a few.

With a passion for training, Karen continues to lead her $ucce$$ Expre$$ Leadership Team to be one of the top teams in Alabama.

She loves to travel and speak with other representatives, on the district and division level, and would love to come to your area to help you achieve your dreams with Avon!

Photo by Lacey Criss

A View from Your Window

BY KATHERYN ANDERSON

A lock handle. That is what they call the little piece of metal you turn to lock a window. You walk around your house looking for one in the "unlock" position, because you are locked out of your house and have no hidden key. No backup plan. You wish you had gotten a spare key made, as your frustration grows with each disappointing discovery. Finally, you find an unlocked window. *Thank goodness!* Now you remove the screen, push up the window, climb through, and successfully enter your home.

During this entire experience, you wished for an unlocked window, wished for a spare key, and wished you remembered your key. You probably did not think about just being grateful for the window.

We take windows for granted, yet they illuminate an otherwise dark room, keep excess noise out, and let fresh air in. Your *belief window* makes all the difference in *your* world. Your belief window is about having expectations.

My Belief Window

The limousine pulled up in front of our home. We had actually done it. My sister and I had earned our Avon® promotions. I reached Senior Executive Unit Leader (SEUL) and she achieved Executive Unit Leader (EUL)—and we did it very fast. In less than two years, I went from a dozen team members to more than 275; from a team that could not hit $1,200 to team sales exceeding $41,000 in a two-week period. It was time for my sister and me to celebrate with our husbands!

It was a challenging road. I assure you there is no secret formula. Like anything worth doing, it is hard work. I did not start out determined to make Avon a career that would take me places no job ever had. I just wanted to give it a try. I had worked several part-time sales jobs, including cosmetics, and thought I might be good at it and earn some extra money. I never knew how instrumental Avon would be in my personal transition from not feeling "good enough" to realizing I already am.

I was teaching high school at the time and loved my job and the students. My ten- and eleven-year-old daughters, Payton and Boston, attended the K-12 school where I taught.

I signed on the line and paid my $10 to join Avon. I thought it was a side job to earn some extra income; however, I soon realized it was mostly for the opportunity to set and achieve goals.

At first, I did not want to recruit and only wanted to sell. I attended a rally and everyone made a big deal about my first order of $795. I did not think about recognition when I was working on it, I just wanted to do the very best I could. I was shocked at how much attention I received. It was at this meeting that I heard other representatives share their stories about their teams. They described how they helped their team members and told of the different experiences they had shared with their teams. Like a flash, the light bulb went on. I could continue doing what I was doing—selling, making money and enjoying it—and I could help others do the same and earn bonuses for doing it! From that point on, I hit the ground running.

> *"I believe I will be successful in my Avon business.*
> *Failure is not an option."*
> **—Jessica Hance, Avon Candidate, Glam Squad team**

Before long, I was doing appointments during my lunch hours, during teacher planning periods and after school. I was teaching, working a part-time job, building my Avon business, and handling housework and parenting. It was tough, and it was time to make a choice and take a leap of faith. I would not be returning to school the next year.

Knowing You are Enough

Back to the limousine. "Do we get to ride too?" Payton asked. I told her she and her sister could ride for a few blocks and then we needed to head to dinner. She and Boston ran to open the door. They jumped up and down, holding hands—extremely excited pre-teen girls. I realized that deep down, I knew I could do it. I had seen this moment awhile back, somewhere in the distance, through my belief window.

Our tuxedo-clad chauffeur waited with the door open as I climbed into the limo with my daughters, whom I can only describe as splendid. As we drove, I looked at them and remembered something from my high school years. We had rented a limo for senior prom. I was decked out in a white sequin dress and perfect make up. My father had called and asked if he could meet me at the restaurant so he could see me in my dress. I was thrilled. I waited in the hotel lobby, outside the restaurant, and saw him stroll through the door. People always noticed him when he arrived; he is 6'4" and usually sports a power suit. He simply told me I was beautiful—not that I *looked* beautiful, that I *was* beautiful. In that moment, I believed him. It was one of the few moments in my young life that I felt I was completely enough, and it felt sublime.

You see, I always felt like people did not think I was good enough. Remember back in grade school how there was always that one kid everybody picked on? I was that kid. The popular girls would not play with me, and the boys called me names. It was nearly crippling. I was fortunate to have a mom who always told me she loved me and that it did not matter what the kids said. For some reason, though, I thought I had to "earn" their approval. I wanted to achieve acceptance, and this poison spilled into many aspects of my life for a long time.

In upper elementary school, the taunting turned into small, random acts of meanness. I was accused of stealing a candy bar from the teacher's desk and was picked last every gym class—even though I was athletic! I was never good enough. Even so, I could see a different picking order through my window.

My life has been a quest that would somehow prove I was worthy— to be enough. Avon not only gave me the time with my family that I desired, it also helped me break out of my self-constructed prison; a constant aching for validation that placed me in figurative shackles.

Helping Others See Themselves Through a Better Window

"In the past—I didn't see a lot in my window; no confidence. With Avon, I grew to believe in myself."
—Jan Keller, Avon Unit Leader, Glam Squad team

Shortly after my resignation from teaching, my sister, Tiffany, called and wanted to know if I would mind if she sold Avon, too. I immediately welcomed her. About six months later, I sat down with her to find out what her goals were. I knew she would be the best business partner I could possibly have. She said, "Let's do this, Sis!" That began the next phase.

We worked day and night and talked to everyone we met. We both had other jobs and kids, worked 12- to 14-hour days, and recruited as many as 28 new representatives in a single campaign. No huge events, no elaborate recruiting endeavors or massive advertising campaigns, just one-on-one conversations with everyone we met about an opportunity we believed in. I remember working every day from January to June without a day off. Sharing the Avon opportunity with so many different people is how the really meaningful stuff started happening.

"After my home was destroyed, my customers' support gave me hope and reasons to never give up."
—Kathy Harter, Avon President's Club, Glam Squad team

I received a "lead share" from Avon. Yes! I had earned the program by recruiting, and now Avon would send me occasional leads. My task was merely to contact them, present the opportunity, and get them started. I immediately called a lead, we'll call her Patience, and she wanted to get started. I set up an appointment to meet with her in a lovely booth—you know, the ones that come with a paper crown and where you can "have it your way." She came through the doors, and I noticed her clothes were dirty and that she could not have been more than 18. She was petite and showed signs of self-neglect.

During the appointment, I made my way through the materials as usual. She apologized for being dirty and proceeded to tell me that a "friend" had stolen her clothes. She had to wear them dirty because they were all the clothes she had. Patience was, in fact, 18 and had just dropped out of high school. She was "dancing" at a club to try to make ends meet. From the minute she walked in, I did not expect her to be my next Avon star, and I would love to end this story with some fascinating turn around or prodigious change. I cannot. However, I did get the chance to tell her that she was valuable; that she had choices and could work to become anything she wanted.

The next time I saw her, I helped her hang fifty books on doors near where she was staying and gave her a bag of my daughters' clothes that they no longer wanted. Soon after that, her phone stopped working and I could no longer reach her. I know I met her for a reason. With Avon, I can impact others so they can see themselves through a better window and expand what they see. You do not always get the chance to witness how much they change the view because of your influence, yet your own belief window gains meaning every time.

I began to realize that what I could accomplish with Avon was so much greater than any title or even myself. Sure, the daily tasks are actually ordinary, mundane. The daily job includes phone calls, fieldwork and consistent follow-up—a series of small habits that build big results. It certainly does not feel grandiose when you are sending emails or stamping brochures. It is the simple things, like reassuring someone that she is significant. That is the real phenomenon.

A Pivotal Moment. A New Window

It was August, and both proverbial and literal sweat dripped. We were headed into the best chance of accomplishing our goals— fourth quarter. We had five new titled leaders and were recruiting with a fury. Campaign 21, 2012, we aimed for $17,500. When we started our crusade, the goal was $15,000, which was raised when we had only two months left on the payout clock. We managed this additional challenge by pressing on with even more determination. I logged on to check the numbers and we did it! I was not even sure it was real.

Tiffany was EUL. I thought this landmark would just feel like the next big step toward SEUL, yet it did not. It felt absolutely complete. If I got no further, that would be okay. It dawned on me that her success was enough. That was a pivotal moment for me. *I* was already enough. Two campaigns later, I hit my numbers too. We had accomplished what we set out to do. I made SEUL and I could not have done it without her.

When others suggested I write a chapter for this book, I almost instinctively thought, *I'm not even a Senior right now, I'm just an Executive.* Then I caught myself. Did I really just entertain that thought? *Just* an Executive? My next thought was, *stop.* I am not *just* an Executive, I am successful. My paradigm has changed and Avon helped alter it. I can finally see all the things through my window that were always there. Fulfillment makes this business special, and in seeking to help others find their belief window, I could finally see through mine.

Pay the Price to Get What You Want

We arrived back home in the limo, and the girls were awaiting our return. I put my arms around my two most precious gifts. The limo's temporary stay ended as quickly as it began, and I knew our future had many more stories to tell. My husband, Charles, is now my co-applicant and takes on many aspects of the business. Together, we can take this business anywhere.

"I can give honest and hard work to others. I believe all I do is ultimately for God's glory."
–Charles Anderson, husband and co-app of Katheryn Anderson

One piece of advice I have shared with my daughters is that everything in life has a price tag. If you want to be the best, then practice more than anyone else. That is the price. If you want to get A's in school, study hard, even when others are having fun. That is the price. If you want to buy what you want, work hard. You get the idea. Do not just choose what you want out of life; decide if you are willing to pay the price tag on it. See it through your belief window, protect it, and do not let anyone rob you of it.

"I am capable. Life is tough, but I am strong."
—Payton Anderson, daughter of Katheryn and Charles Anderson

"I am loved. I am a hard worker."
—Boston Anderson, daughter of Katheryn and Charles Anderson

In your Avon business, do not think about what you are trying to achieve as some mythical end of the road or you will never feel like you arrived. The arrival is not the real prize. The real prize is the beauty you experience along the way. The unobtainable pinnacle does not exist, and you might miss the meaningful experiences that are cumulatively the manifestation of the dream itself.

What Is in Your Belief Window?

I have experienced failures and accomplishments, yet I am always a success. That is how I see myself in the distance, through my window.

"When I started Avon, my window was picturesque. The only problem was my view was blocked by the kids' dirty handprints. The need to fulfill my role as a mother clouded my vision. Then I realized Avon was what my family needed. Now my window is sparkling clean, and I see that I can be a great mom and have amazing income potential."
—Tiffany Schoenauer, Katheryn Anderson's sister and Avon Advanced Unit Leader, Glam Squad team

My challenge to you is to see what is in your belief window, not what others see. Writing it down is the first step to wherever you want to go. I could explain our exact plan, our strategies and methods, which I share at many seminars; however, until you Windex® your window of expectations about who you are and what you can accomplish, all of that is irrelevant.

As you plan your success, access your deep-seated strength. It is the fuel that will sustain you. In this business, you will experience frequent setbacks and disappointments. Manage them and keep your Windex on hand! When you see yourself for all you are capable of accomplishing—it is a beautiful view of you.

KATHERYN ANDERSON

Avon® Executive Unit Leader

Glam Squad Team/Honor Society
Creator of Movin' Up Materials
515-975-7544
avon.katianderson@gmail.com
www.youravon.com/kanderson5754
www.allaboutrealglam.com

Sharing her gift of teaching is Katheryn's (Kati's) calling and fulfills her desire to help others. She is a former high school teacher, tumbling and trampoline coach and gym owner, and has worked in cosmetics since 1989. Today, Kati applies her teaching abilities to working with her customers and her team.

Kati uses motivational speaking to share her recruiting and training expertise. She creates and uses her original materials to enhance the learning experiences of her representatives and leaders. She connects with other women on www.allaboutrealglam.com, a website designed to emphasize inner beauty and empowerment. Her accomplishments in building her team earned her the Recruiting Excellence Award for the Shining Stars Divisions in 2013 and 2014. She received #1 in the region for team growth in 2012, and her team performed at $750,000 in sales in less than two years growth. Kati is a member of the DSWA and recipient of her district's 2012 Spirit of Avon Award.

Kati holds a teaching degree from Iowa State University. In addition to homeschooling her children, she teaches a speech and college prep writing class. She resides with her husband and her two daughters in Urbandale, Iowa.

Photo by K & K Smith Photography

Dream It...Believe It... Achieve It!

BY SUZY ISHMAEL

When I was in fifth grade, my teacher asked, "What would you like to do when you grow up?" I clearly remember saying, "I want to be the boss and would like to go to Hawaii." That was my dream!

A lady used to come to our house every month to show us items from her bag. My mom would always buy the small, burgundy jar of body lotion. To this day, Imari® remains her favorite scent. At the time, I had no concept about Avon®.

My older brother, younger sister and I did not always have everything we wanted when we were growing up in Trinidad. My mother was a seamstress and my dad was a driver. They both worked hard to provide for our needs.

My father's side of the family lived in the United States and my parents would travel back and forth during my teen years to provide a better life. Being the older sister, my responsibilities exceeded that of a typical teenager. I would make extra money by sewing and babysitting in the neighborhood.

We planned to move to the United States once we finished school. However, after completing my education in business management I started working in the oil industry at age 18. Our plan to move seemed most unlikely. Ten years later, my parents moved back to Trinidad permanently.

> *"Even when you think you have your life all mapped out,*
> *things happen that shape your destiny in ways you*
> *might never have imagined."*
> **—Deepak Chopra, Indian-American author,**
> **public speaker and physician**

Someone on ICQ, the social media at the time, mistook me for someone else with the same name. In responding to him, I discovered that he was also born in Trinidad and had moved to the United States to follow his dreams as a musician and songwriter. When Shazad traveled back to Trinidad to visit his family, we met and it was love at first sight. The rest is history. I still cannot comprehend what transpired in that one week. Shazad proposed in two days, and two days later we had an engagement party. We got married one hour later! The next thing I knew I was on a flight to New York.

I moved into my husband's one-bedroom apartment on Staten Island, New York. I saw that my work was cut out for me—it was definitely a man cave.

A couple of months later, we learned I was pregnant. I was both scared and excited. It was yet another life change in a year of so many, and I had no family or friends around. I spent many lonely nights reminiscing about the life I had left behind.

That winter, we welcomed our baby boy, Saleem. We needed more living space, and I needed a job to supplement my husband's income in order to move from our apartment.

Soon I received two job offers. The higher paying job was in the World Trade Center and the other was on the island. I accepted the job closer to home to be available for my son in case of an emergency. I became an executive assistant for AVSP, an agency for the developmentally disabled.

We found a two-family house in our neighborhood, made the down payment with all our savings, and moved in that summer. My husband worked nights, which was a blessing, since we could not afford babysitting. This way we could juggle our time for our son.

Six months later, tragedy hit the World Trade Center and more than 2,000 people lost their lives in a terrorist attack. All I could think of was that I could have been one of them if I had chosen the higher-paying job.

We had a thirty-year mortgage. I could not believe we would have to work until we were sixty just to pay it. My parents had never had credit cards and always lived within their means. I had that same mentally, and the debt on a house concerned me.

Looking for Answers

"It doesn't matter who you are, or where you come from. The ability to triumph begins with you always."
—Oprah Winfrey, American talk show host, actress, producer and philanthropist

My quest for a way to live debt free began. Our income was insufficient for the lifestyle we wanted. We decided to refinance for a shorter period with a goal of paying off our mortgage by the time I turned forty. Our payment doubled, yet our salaries remained the same. I needed to find some answers.

When It All Started

"Dreams are your paint; the world is your canvas. Believing is the brush that converts your dreams into a masterpiece of reality."
—Author unknown

A local flea market operated on the weekends near my home, which sparked an idea I thought might solve our problem. It looked like a perfect place to start a business while working my full-time job. No one was selling beauty supplies, so I saw a gap and thought of Avon. My husband was on board and I applied online. The next thing I knew, an Avon lady was at my door to sign me up. I occasionally bought Avon products before and never realized how simple it would be to sell them.

There were many times in our first year when I wanted to quit. Renting space and purchasing products upfront was a financial strain. My husband's constant reminders that I was spending more than I made did not make it any easier.

Making It Happen

"If you don't go after what you want, you'll never have it.
If you don't ask, the answer is always no. If you don't step forward,
you're always in the same place."
—Nora Roberts, American bestselling author

During my second year in Avon, I was at a sales meeting when my District Sales Manager (DSM) had us create dream boards. At first I thought it was silly; however, my dream board still hangs on my wall today, displaying pictures of $1 million in Monopoly® money, a baby girl, a brick house, a Jacuzzi® and hula girls.

Two years after creating my dream board, I found out I was pregnant. For my birthday we welcomed our baby girl, Sarah. A goal from my dream board had come true, proving it really worked. It was time to take action for the other items on my dream board.

I decided to learn everything I could about Avon by attending sales meetings and online trainings. My clientele grew to more than 2,000 customers. By providing excellent service, you gain repeat customers and consistently increase sales.

Sarah was not even a year old when the flea market decided to close its doors to the public after 16 years. I had a lot of inventory and did not know what I was going to do. The local newspaper interviewed me and I remember saying, "I am nervous, but I think everything happens for a reason. This may be a blessing in disguise and a chance for a new opportunity." One month later, I rented a storefront property and embarked on a new journey; I opened an Avon Licensed Beauty Center.

Making Dreams Come True

"There exists only one person who has the power to cast the deciding vote that will kill your dreams—you!"
—Dr. Robert Schuller, American retired televangelist, pastor, motivational speaker and author

My girlfriend, Laura, and I attended our first Avon conference in Connecticut in 2012, where we bonded as Avon sisters. Until then, I did not understand the leadership part and saw no point in working that angle of the business, but we became highly motivated after hearing top senior leadership representatives tell their success stories and we joked about going on stage to share our own. This year I had the honor of being a guest speaker at the Avon Conference in Orlando, Florida.

I had not paid attention to Avon incentives until the Bon Jovi incentive in Las Vegas. I am a die-hard Bon Jovi fan. I made sure to earn the trip along with two of my team members. Avon certainly delivered its promise and the concert was beyond my expectations. We had the fifth row from center stage. It was great meeting other representatives from around the country. One of my "wow" moments was meeting the legendary Lisa Wilber.

Little did I know there was more to come.

> *"People begin to become successful*
> *the minute they decide to be."*
> **—Harvey Mackay, American businessman**
> **and best selling author**

Later that year, my personal sales rocketed to over $112,000. I achieved President's Council and earned a trip to Hawaii *(the hula girls from my dream board.)* My husband and I made it the long overdue honeymoon we never had. We were able to pay off our mortgage three months prior to my 41st birthday, and later that year we bought our second dream house and installed a Jacuzzi tub. My dream board had come to life before my eyes.

Now I work both angles of my business—sales and leadership. I won the Advanced Unit Leader (AUL) Academy scholarship with Laura.

Two days before Christmas, my DSM called to tell me Laura had died that day. While visiting her family for the holidays, she collapsed and died from a brain aneurysm. I was totally devastated. It was so unfair. She was only 51 years old.

Just days before Laura's death, she and I had promised each other we would make Executive Unit Leader (EUL). This gave me great determination and I graduated in 2014 as an EUL—for both Laura and me. After being stuck at the AUL level for six years, I was beyond ecstatic.

The year 2014 was also great because, through Avon, we earned the "Catch the Magic Incentive" for my entire family and we were able to celebrate my daughter's fourth birthday in Disney World®.

> *"All our dreams can come true, if we have
> the courage to pursue them."*
> **—Walt Disney, American business magnate,
> cartoonist and filmmaker**

My team sold over $1 million dollars in Avon products, fulfilling my entire dream board. It does not stop there. My new dream board now hangs next to the old one as a reminder that hard work and believing in yourself makes all the difference.

My new dream board shows that I intend to achieve Senior Executive Unit Leader rank, supplement my income from my other job, travel to Europe, send my children to college, and purchase a vacation house in the Caribbean.

The lifetime friendships I have built with my team members surpass any monetary gain. They are my second family. We share personal struggles and successes. My greatest satisfaction has been the ability to change lives by doing what I love and seeing the amazing, life-changing results.

The confidence and knowledge I have acquired from my business have transferred to my personal life. I can live by example for my children and transfer a valuable legacy to them.

I now work part time at my other job, and I can enjoy spending more time with my family. We have traveled and enriched our lives in many ways that would not have been possible without Avon.

Advice for Success

"Success is the sum of small efforts, repeated day in and day out."
—Robert Collier, American author

I often hear, "What's the secret?" or "You're so lucky!" There is no secret and it is not luck. It is hard work and you make the choices that decide your future. Here are twelve success strategies:

1. Define your goals. Write them down or they are only wishes. Visualize them and they can come to life.

2. Have determination. Focus on what works. Find solutions not excuses. Quitting is not an option.

3. Use a daily planner. Plan your day the night before and you will wake up knowing where to start.

4. Take advantage of social media and technology. These tools enable you to continuously reach new goals. Be consistent in promoting your website. Remember to also keep the lines of personal communication open because they are vital for defining you and your connections.

5. Use Avon products. Be your own walking billboard and testimony. Let your business become part of you and your everyday life so the world recognizes you every time you walk out your door.

6. Be involved. My DSM guidance and support has been a huge motivator in my continued success. Attend conferences, sales meetings and trainings. Listen and learn from the leaders before you. You can monetize their techniques and success stories.

7. Communicate. Statistics show communication with new representatives is of utmost importance for their success.

8. Use Avon's sales tools. Use all that Avon has to offer, from their Downline Manager, Pathways and PRP Tracking to their Campaign Planning Tools.

9. Be a good leader. You cannot lead someone further than you have gone yourself. Being the best at what you do and duplicating that process to help others achieve their goals makes you soar.

10. Identify team members' needs. Work with them individually on their strengths and weaknesses. The results may surprise you. Divide the task and multiply the success.

11. Embrace positivity. Surround yourself with people who inspire and challenge you. Be around those who see the greatness within you, even when you do not see it yourself.

12. Be true to yourself. When you find that passion to do what you love, it does not feel like work!

"Even the greatest was once a beginner.
Don't be afraid to take that first step."
—Author unknown

You can make your dreams come true if you vividly imagine them, sincerely believe in yourself, and take action with enthusiasm and determination to succeed.

Avon's name is known worldwide for its reputation of empowering women globally. You can benefit from that name recognition. All you have to do is embrace the opportunity and believe in your success.

I am forever grateful to God for all my blessings. I could not have imagined what a wonderful life I would have with my husband and beautiful children. No words can express my gratitude to my parents and family for their love and support and to Avon for the unlimited opportunities they provide.

> *"Many of life's failures are people who did not realize how close they were to success when they gave up."*
> **—Thomas A. Edison, American inventor and businessman**

By reading this book, you have already taken one step forward. The choices you make determine your destiny. Dream It...Believe It... Achieve It! Embrace the Avon opportunity. I encourage you to use the strategies here and take that journey with me to success. See you at the top.

SUZY ISHMAEL

Avon® Executive Unit Leader
President's Council Member
Licensed Avon Beauty Center
718-619-3396 /718-619-7250
suzy.ishmael@gmail.com
www.sellavon.com Code: SI
www.youravon.com/si

Suzy was born in Trinidad and Tobago. She majored in business studies and worked in the oil industry by age 18. After marrying and moving to the United States, she started working for a not-for-profit agency that provides services for the developmentally disabled.

Suzy began selling Avon in 2007 to increase her income and become debt free. She graduated from AUL Academy and advanced to Executive Unit Leader with a team that has earned over $1,000,000 in unit sales. She has achieved President's Council level with over $112,000 in personal sales, making her #1 for Top Seller and Leadership titles in her district. In 2011, Suzy opened a Licensed Avon Beauty Center (LABC), the only Avon store on Staten Island, serving the New York area.

Suzy and her husband, Shazad, have two children, Saleem and Sarah. When the entire family is not helping with the Avon business, Suzy loves spending time with them and cheering on her husband and son as they make their music dreams comes true. The family enjoyed an Avon incentive trip to Disney World in 2014. Suzy's passion is sharing the Avon opportunity and helping empower women to make their dreams come true.

What's Important:
Excuses or Success?

BY REBECCA SPUEHLER

I grew up as the middle child in a house of five kids and have a half sister. My mom is from Mexico and brought us up with a lot of Mexican culture. Although I did not finish high school or get a formal education, my parents taught me all the basics. I learned to love and care for my brothers and sisters and to work hard. I learned that courtesy costs nothing. My dad taught us to be strong, and my mom taught us to love the Lord.

I have two boys. My first son, Tony, and I have been through many challenges together—God bless him. I made a lot of bad choices when he was little and put him through a lot. Among other things, we were homeless for a while. However, I chose life with my Lord instead of death and started fighting for our lives.

My second son, Marcus, stepped into our lives when he was five and a half. Although I am not Marcus' birth-mother, my heart does not know that.

I went to beauty college and enjoyed giving manicures for years while we lived in Nevada. After we moved to California, I worked different jobs. I decided to try real estate and met people who changed my life. I met Robert Dorsey and we became a strong team, listing and selling the most homes together. As time went on, we became more than work partners; we became life partners!

I also met Dan and Jackie Mundy at the agency, and we all sold homes together. I was young and dumb when I met them—about 27 years old. Imagine sweet Jackie working next to me, a girl who wore mini dresses, smoked, drank and cursed. What a mess I was.

Avon. Do I Have To?

I began having heart problems, and I stopped selling real estate. I had to have surgery and needed to take it easy. I decided to do childcare at my house, which really was not taking it easy.

Then Dan told Robert about Avon. Robert brought the kit home and said, "Look what you are doing." I was less than enthusiastic, as we had already been involved with other businesses, and I was tired. I did not want one more thing to do.

I agreed to join because I realized I could purchase my products at a discount. I had a couple of customers: my mom, sister and best friend. Dan and Jackie sent books and materials home with Robert for me; however, I only stashed them behind the couch or threw them away. My manager came by once, and I never saw her again.

A few months later, Dan told me I had a new manager who wanted to get together with me. I avoided Dan because I knew his plan would come with work and obligation. After all, I had things to do. I needed to jump-start my car to pick my son up from school. I needed to have a yard sale to make money to buy him birthday presents.

Kathy, another Avon representative, would pick up orders and encourage me to put an order in. I could not get it together. I was removed at least 13 times and never paid my bill on time. My manager would beg me to at least put a mascara order in. I did not want to order books because they would end up in the garbage. Kathy would harass me to go to the meetings and offered to pick me up and drop me off. I told her I absolutely did not want to talk to anybody or stand up in front of a room full of people. When she said they had treats and coffee at these meetings, I began to show up. It was instant love between me and the manager, Jan, who asked me to join her support team.

The Shiny Broach

One day Jan held up a big, gaudy broach during our group meeting. She told us that whoever brings in five recruits could win it. I did not have much and loved costume jewelry. To me, winning a broach would be like getting gold or a new car. I was extremely excited. I recruited my sister, my best friend and my mom. Jan told us to knock on doors to recruit anybody we could.

Dan explained to our manager that if I did the recruiting, I could be successful. He and Jackie saw things in me that I did not see in myself. I took the books out of the garbage and started knocking on doors and recruiting, which was scary at first. I prayed nobody would answer the door. I just wanted to sneak up to doors, drop off books, and leave quietly. Still, I wanted people to say yes, because I desperately wanted that beautiful, gaudy broach—and I managed to win it!

My business started to develop. I did not realize then that a giant was growing. Jackie and Dan encouraged my manager and me, and they were always there when I needed them. Jackie asked me what I wanted and talked about goals and growing my business, which scared me.

Jan dangled the proverbial carrot in front of me, and I was hopping like a rabbit for my business. I would cut out pictures of the rewards I wanted from brochures and glue them onto a piece of paper. She would write down how many people I would have to recruit to earn those items. I worked my tail off.

My unit was growing and so were the checks. I was enjoying all the clothing and jewelry I earned. Everybody likes to work hard to earn things!

A Family Effort

My family was involved in helping with the business. My boys helped with events and went on their bikes and skates to canvas with me. Robert scrutinized what I was doing. He wanted to know how much I paid for the books, what customer returns were costing, where dinner was, and why I needed the car.

Keep in mind that I started with only three recruits—my mom, my sister and my best friend. Now I wanted to recruit everybody. When my first customer called at 8:45 p.m., Robert answered and I heard him say on the phone, "Do you know what time it is?" I was mortified. I flew over the couch like a gazelle to grab the phone out of his hand.

Another time, I had to deliver on a military base to a first-time customer. I promised she would have the order that night. Robert was late getting home with the junker—our car—and took me to drop off the order. Then I discovered that the base gate closed at 8:00 p.m. I was already half an hour late and still determined to make the delivery. I talked Robert into hoisting me up over the wall! I walked another 45 minutes to her house and made sure she received her order. She was unhappy that I was late and never called me again. Still, I kept my word.

Robert did not take my business seriously because he did not see that money could be made. I assure you that you can make money with Avon. I made $1,800 my first year. My first leadership bonus check was $1.86. Then it continued to grow.

Goals and Breakfast; the Magic Words

Jackie continued to try to pin me down to do goal setting and wanted me to meet with her and our upline, Vondell McKenzie. I attended their motivating leadership meetings, where I met Vondell's husband, Terry. He introduced himself as my grandfather in the Avon business, which warmed my heart. Eventually, Jackie invited me to breakfast with her and Vondell. I was hesitant to go because I did not know how to set goals; however, Jackie mentioned breakfast, and those were the magic words. We enjoyed a wonderful breakfast, and they helped me figure out the important things in my life and turn them into goals. I thought I would leave breakfast with the goal of being an Advanced Unit Leader (AUL). Instead, I left with a goal of becoming an Executive Unit Leader (EUL). It was a four-month plan, and I did it in five.

My business was thriving. I advanced to EUL, and when Robert saw that I had earned $45,000 that year, it became our business.

My dreams started to come true because of my Avon business. I set goals for everything I did. Dan challenged me to set a goal of hitting Senior Executive Unit Leader (SEUL). We also competed to see who could develop four Executives first—Dan or me. The loser would pay for a trip to Europe for the other one. I won!

Dan and Jackie took us on a trip to France that I will never forget. After that, life really started changing for us. I was able to purchase my dream home, buy cars and go on trips. We were all working hard and growing our business with earnings of almost a quarter of a million dollars a year!

From Tragedy to New Beginnings

Then tragedy hit our home. Robert was in a near-fatal car accident and we thought he was going to die. We prayed and waited while he was in a coma for a month and stayed in the hospital for several months. Tony maintained the business while I spent all my time at the hospital.

I cannot think of any other job in which you could endure a horrific life tragedy, not knowing when you will return to work, and still continue to receive checks every two weeks. Avon did that for me! They were right there alongside me, caring, praying and visiting. Robert recovered after three years of rehabilitation. Unfortunately, nothing was the same after that. Our personal life and our business took a hit.

After struggling through five years of hard times, Robert and I needed to go our separate ways. I had to start a new life and rebuild my Avon business. I leaned on my faith, my Avon family around me, the training Avon had provided, my manager, my family and my friends. The great thing about Avon is that anytime and anywhere is a good time to start or rebuild an Avon business.

I became a Certified Beauty Adviser Trainer through Avon and still use those skills daily. Avon had me doing a lot of speaking engagements, training events and boot camps. This increased my confidence and ability to train my own team. I have spoken at many Avon conferences. Although I feel scared every time I speak, I do it because I am passionate about my business and love the representatives. I now offer training, skin care, makeup, and leadership classes.

You, too, can have a successful Avon business. I encourage you to use the tools Avon provides. Identify your goals by figuring out what is important to you. If your parents are important to you, decide how you want to help them, and set a goal. If your grandchildren are important to you, discover their needs, and set a goal to provide for them. If your business is lacking something, figure out what that is, and set a goal to resolve it.

Build your relationship with Avon, the people and the products. You are the face of Avon, and it is imperative that you take the time to train, attend meetings and explore the products. You must become one with Avon.

Passion and Belief

Have a belief system. I believe in God first, and I believe he will guide me all the way. In 2011, I married my high school sweetheart, Victor Alejandre, a wonderful man whom I adore. What I love the most about him is the way he loves the Lord and then me. In 2013, Victor gave up his business as an electrician to help me with my Avon business. We now have two training centers.

I believe in Avon—an incredible company. I am grateful for my team of representatives and hard-working managers. I believe in and honor my family and friends who love and encourage me. I am truly blessed! What do you believe in? How far will you stretch to achieve your goals and dreams?

I am proud to always hit President's Club and recently hit Rose Circle. I always cry when I receive my Mrs. Albee Award and I adore the President's Club luncheons. I love going on all the trips, where I get to see my precious Avon family. I pray for all of you, as you are always in my heart. Please let me know if you need extra prayer.

I think that becoming a President's Club member should be everybody's dream and goal. I also encourage you to try leadership. If you are going to give something a try, then give it the best you have got—100 percent. Do it right, ask for help, watch to see what others are doing, and believe in yourself. It all starts with trying.

I watched and followed top sellers in my district; I worked with other representatives, some of whom were not even in my downline. I learned from all of these people, including the Mundys and the McKenzies.

Final Thoughts

I have been through a lot of turmoil in my life, from domestic violence, to substance abuse, to rehabilitation, to low self-esteem, to homelessness. I could have made many excuses to fail. Instead, I stopped that poisonous thinking and decided to discover reasons to become a success. You get to choose which way you want to go—excuses or success!

Tidbits

You are your best advertisement. Make the best first impression you can and sell yourself.

Your customers are the heart of your business. Treat them like queens and kings.

Take advantage of everything Avon offers. Use the Internet, your own website, managers and training. Work with both sales and with leadership.

Connect with social media. If you do not know how to use social media, then find someone to help. Chances are your children or grandchildren are experts who can teach you.

Build relationships with your team members. Give them basic tools, point them in the right direction, show them these lessons, and pray! Let them know they can have the same results as you.

We all go through seasons and can thrive. Are you making excuses or choosing success?

REBECCA SPUEHLER

Avon® National Senior Executive Unit Leader

916-331-1001
rebeccasavonworld@gmail.com
www.youravon.com/rdorsey

Rebecca and her husband, Victor Alejandre, live in Sacramento, California. They have a team of over 1,000 people and two training centers. Their successful business continues to grow and Rebecca focuses on helping others be the best they can be and on treating her clients like kings and queens.

Rebecca has earned numerous Avon awards and has had roles in training videos. She has been a speaker at many events and a beauty advisor trainer. Rebecca is a member of many council groups and is featured in *Avon Dreams* magazine. She has hosted boot camps and earned Avon trips. She has been featured on television, in People® magazine, and in several newspapers. Despite having minimal education and no professional training, Rebecca found opportunities through Avon to become financially independent, empowered, confident, brave, outgoing, secure, educated and worthy.

Rebecca and Victor pray, play and work together. They are involved in their church and doing work for the Lord. Rebecca goes on a missionary trip once a year. They enjoy spending time with their children, grandson Tyler, and their two dogs and one cat.

Thank you, Shan Drum, for your kind heart and willingness to help me write my story.

Rekindling the
Entrepreneurial Spark

BY WENDY McGEHRIN

Growing up in University Park, Maryland, with my older sister and my parents, my small family always supported my adventures, even from a young age. Although my family was highly educated, I did not enjoy school and always felt like the black sheep of the family. Lacking the confidence to pursue a higher education, I held myself back and feared failure.

However, there were two things that gave me great joy from an early age—feeling appreciated for what I created and the positive attention I received when entertaining others. This led to the development of my entrepreneurial spirit.

My neighbors used to watch me perform shows on our front porch, and they even paid admission. At age 18, I sold Avon® briefly for the first time, as well as selling my crafts. Meeting new people at craft shows was part of the excitement and made my entrepreneurial spirit soar. I had a gift for selling, and it came easily to me. People trusted me for being upfront and honest about anything I promoted. If I did not absolutely love a product myself, I did not recommend it. I never thought of myself as a "sales person," just someone who loves to help others get what they want.

At age 23 I married Tim. It was one of the happiest days of my life. I was working as a secretary, but continued to experience the thrill of making and selling my ceramic crafts. That was when I gave Avon a second chance. However, life became a bit more challenging when, after 11 years of marriage, my husband died of heart failure due to complications from long-term diabetes. Our two beautiful daughters were only 3 and 5 years old. I left my job as a secretary to be with my girls and started working in another home-based business.

Soon, my world suddenly stopped again. My youngest daughter, Ann—who was then five years old, was diagnosed with leukemia. Getting the news was like being kicked in the gut. We spent 11 terrifying days in the hospital for her initial treatments to stabilize her condition before beginning her scary, three-year-long journey with chemotherapy.

Clearly, it was a time to put on my big girl pants and do what I needed to do for my family. I was broke, yet needed to be there for my daughters. For the next several years, we made many long drives to the children's hospital for Ann's treatments. After five years, it was such a relief to be told that Ann was in complete remission and cured. Today, both my daughters are living healthy, adult lives.

To make a little extra money for my family during Ann's recovery, I signed up with Avon for a third time. Initially, I still did not see the huge opportunity Avon offered. That began to change as Ann's health improved and I could devote more time to my growing business. As they say, "The third time is the charm." I was finally ready to jump into Avon with both feet. I was no longer just in it to get discounts on my personal purchases. I was selling again, and with support from family and neighbors, I rediscovered my entrepreneurial spark that I had in childhood. I finally realized that, ironically, Avon was the perfect business opportunity which had been there waiting for me all along!

The Turning Point of Success

Before Avon, I was dirt broke. I would worry about spending even one dollar frivolously. Worse, I worried constantly about losing our home. All of that began to change as I grew more serious about my Avon business. It was not easy, yet things were starting to move in the right direction.

A major turning point was meeting meeting successful representatives. I met Lisa Wilber at an Avon convention in Dallas, Texas. I was surprised to learn that highly successful people were normal people like me. I began to believe that I, too, could have that kind of success. I remember talking to Lisa and handing her my business card with a note saying, "See you at the top."

At that first convention, I had already achieved Unit Leader and was bound and determined to make a go of it. My first Unit Leader check was only $50, and I needed to earn ten times that much. Although I achieved President's Club during my first year, finances were still tight. This motivated me to set a much bigger goal, and I never looked back.

I started using the "Power of three," which meant setting a goal of meeting several new people each day. I made a daily routine of talking to complete strangers wherever possible and was able to recruit many new customers and new team members as a result. I enjoyed these interactions whether we discussed Avon or not. When I offered the Avon opportunity and shared what it had done for me, it never felt like work. Living in Lincoln, Delaware, with its population of only 7,400 residents, has not held me back from succeeding in this business. When I would go to the local Walmart® and other stores, I would only know a few people out of the hundreds who were shopping and saw that as a huge opportunity to meet new people!

The Great Life with Avon

Sometimes I feel almost guilty because this lifestyle—not having a boss and setting my own schedule—is too much fun to be called work! I love the awesome feeling of freedom to do what I love, like going to the beach on a weekday. Sometimes I take work with me and sit on the beach making calls while enjoying the beautiful day—the best office in town. The best part is feeling empowered to do the things you never thought possible. I am continually learning to dream bigger. I have a plan of action and set goals to make my dreams come true.

Avon has afforded me many great opportunities with fun and rewarding incentives. Each time Avon offered a prize or incentive I set a goal and figured out how to earn it. There is no stopping me once my eye is on a prize. My favorite was an all-expenses-paid trip to Jamaica for two. I have earned many other great prizes over the years. I earned a Keurig® Coffee System, a full-size iPad®, a 46-inch television, and a $2,000 cash bonus—to name just a few.

I admit that I have missed targets when I failed to form an action plan. Most recently, I regret missing the 2014 Avon Convention in Orlando, Florida. Distractions are a constant danger that can detour any action plan. Failure, however, has actually supercharged my motivation. Nothing will stop me now from getting to Senior Executive Unit Leader.

My life with Avon is much easier now than when I first started. I now consistently earn at least twice my initial goal—enough to easily pay my bills. I am free from worry and can even purchase the little extras here and there.

During the last year of my father's life, my Avon business gave me the freedom to visit him several times a week, driving two and a half hours each way. I spent a lot of quality time with him that year and was able to continue working my business even during our visits. This would not have been possible had I been working a regular job. In fact, I likely would have gotten fired for spending that much time away. Over the years, my father had always come to my rescue. When he became sick, it seemed as if he was holding on to life to protect me. I wanted him to be proud of me and, through what I achieved with Avon, I know that he was. My last words to my dad before he died were, "I will be okay."

Personal Growth Through Business

Helping others by sharing the Avon opportunity is an awesome feeling. With no formal education, I have become successful in something I have always enjoyed: meeting people and selling them what they want and love.

Success brings confidence. Although it has been a struggle, I work on growing my confidence every day. Having a great support team of representatives who look up to me, I am motivated to demonstrate that if I can do it, they can too.

One way this business gives me confidence is by motivating me to push through uncomfortable situations. Going out and prospecting used to be uncomfortable. Now it is second nature. I simply call it *talking*, not prospecting, and that makes it so much easier. You build confidence by doing something repeatedly. If you can be friendly, you can do this business. It is a people business, and if you love people, it is fun and provides limitless opportunities.

It never feels like work. Shopping for clothes is not work, is it? Well, in Avon it is. You can easily bridge a conversation about clothes to a conversation about Avon. For instance, I could be talking about an outfit I'm trying on, or one that someone next to me is admiring, and transition that into how Avon has the perfect piece of jewelry to accessorize it. And often, I will actually be wearing the jewelry to show them right then and there! Sometimes this conversation begins just because I'm wearing an Avon button or name badge.

Business Growth Success Strategies

When I first started my business, I had no idea what I was doing and had no real mentor to show me the way. I learned on my own and unnecessarily reinvented the wheel. I was stubborn and needed to learn the hard way, which took longer. I do not recommend you go that route. There are plenty of great leaders and managers willing to help you become successful. Take advantage of their support and learn from them.

You can achieve your goals and make your dreams come true with a few proven strategies. Every day, I start with a routine. I check my to-do list, check my email, and then check on team members using Avon's Downline Manager.

Working with your team is very important when building a successful business. When I check on my team members, I:

• Check on members who are close to achieving their goals
• Recognize members for various accomplishments
• Check on those who have missed placing their current order
• Complete a call-to-action plan each day

Remember, you are the boss. However, you must do the work or you will be a boss making no money. You need to take your business seriously and work every day, even if it is your part-time job.

I experienced a huge turning point when I started attending events. It took me six months to even consider going to a district meeting. When a friend in Avon mentioned how much fun they were and told me I might even learn something—and maybe win something—I decided to attend. Now I encourage my team to do the same. These meetings provide a lot of valuable information to help me and my team achieve their goals.

Everything I do with my business is charted and easy to follow. Even my fiancé, Brian, understands my business charts. Without them, I have no system.

Here are Four Key Elements that have Helped Me Succeed

1. Keep a customer list. This ensures that you give a brochure to each customer every campaign and miss no one. I work with more than 200 customers on a regular basis. Following up with each one is also an essential step to making more money. I remind my team to do this every campaign.

2. Work with team members who want to work. I have pushed and pulled too many representatives to the finish line. It does not work. However, the power of suggestion helps. That is where Avon's Downline Manager comes into action. When I see representatives close to a certain level, I reach out and ask if they would be interested in growing their own team to reach even higher levels. Everybody is different and their goals are, too. Set a good example, offer advice, and follow through with what you say you will do.

3. Support team members. You can help them go a long way in their businesses. Answer phone calls or return them as soon as possible. There is nothing worse than someone calling in response to an ad and leaving a message, and then not hearing from the representative for hours or days. When someone is excited about starting a business, you need to reach out quickly to help them before their excitement wears off—and it will.

4. Stay organized. Forward your phone calls from your home phone to your cell phone to avoid missing calls. I also recommend that you keep your calendar at your fingertips. Scheduling your personal and Avon time is a fine balance that you can accomplish with a simple calendar. I personally use my calendar on my smart phone and keep it close at hand.

I am so glad I found Avon and gave it a serious chance the third time it came calling. I hope I have inspired you to do the same. With Avon, your dreams really can come true.

This is not a get-rich-quick scheme. Building a successful business requires work. If you put in time every day, you will succeed. You are closer than you think. Work with your mentors, stay focused and organized, and never, never give up.

WENDY McGEHRIN

Avon® Executive Unit Leader
Rose Circle
Leader of Avon Star Climbers
877-337-EARN (3276)
makingchanges@juno.com
www.youravon.com/wendy
www.startavon.com code: Wendy

Wendy was a born entrepreneur who entertained neighbors as a child and sold crafts as a young adult. She eventually carried on her passion for business as an adult with Avon.

Wendy enjoys helping others grow to achieve their dreams and goals. She leads a team of more than 200 representatives in her downline, generating more than $800,000 annually in team sales. With hard work and determination, Wendy has reached a level with Avon at which she earns more than enough to support her family.

Wendy is a member of the Chamber of Commerce in Milford, Delaware, and Rehoboth Beach, Delaware, making networking connections. She is a widow and raised two daughters. In her free time, Wendy enjoys spending time with her fiancé, Brian, and working on home improvement projects. Also, she loves reading and relaxing on the beach, going out to eat, and going to the movies.

More A View From the Top
Volume 3

Now that you have been inspired by our stories and have learned a wide variety of tips, techniques and strategies to build a thriving direct selling or entrepreneurial business; the next step is to take action. Get started applying what you have learned in the pages of this book.

We want you to know that we are here to help you meet your professional and personal objectives. Below is a list of where we are geographically located.

You can find out more about each of us by reading our bios at the end of our chapters, or by visiting our websites listed on the next pages. When you call or email us, let us know you have read our book. We are here to serve you to enjoy your own view from the top!

Geographical Listings for *A View From the Top Volume 3*: Avon's elite leaders share their stories and strategies to succeed

Canada

Ontario
Feanny Xu   www.feannyxu.com

United States

Alabama
Karen Criss   www.youravon.com/kcriss

Arizona
Dolly and Henry Aspeytia   www.youravon.com/daspeytia

California
Theresa Kraai   www.youravon.com/tkraai
Rebecca Spuehler   www.youravon.com/rdorsey

Delaware
Wendy McGehrin   www.youravon.com/wendy

Florida
Lisa Monoson   www.yourbeautylady.com
Heather Murray   www.youravon.com/hmurray

Georgia
Julie Lee Hoffman   www.youravon.com/jh
S. Diane Melton   www.youravon.com/melton

Iowa
Katheryn Anderson   www.youravon.com/kanderson5754

New York
Dilenia Collado   www.youravon.com/dcollado
Suzy Ishmael   www.youravon.com/si

North Carolina
Malcolm and Mary Shelton   www.youravon.com/mshelton

Pennsylvania
Brian and Joanna Neiderhiser   www.youravon.com/jneiderhiser

Tennessee
Susan Roper   www.youravon.com/sroper

Utah
Berta Bench   www.youravon.com/bbench

Virginia
Linda Montavon   www.youravon.com/yes
Jennett Cenname Pulley   www.youravon.com/jpulley

You're Invited...

. . .to join us for the **Business Breakthrough Summit** designed to give you tools to catapult your business growth.

The Business Breakthrough Summit is the right program for you if you want to create new streams of income, are ready to establish yourself as an expert in your field and are looking for a way of easily doing both. It is time for you to be one of the influential people in your field.

Join us at the Business Breakthrough Summit and in one weekend, you will gain the information and tools you need to accelerate your ability to easily add clients and learn how to be loud and proud about the value you bring to the marketplace.

Find out more about our next live event at: www.bizbreakthrough. com. Because you picked up and read this book, it is clear you have business savvy, therefore we have a gift for you. Enter coupon code BBSVIP50 for a 50% discount on your registration. Attend this event and watch your business thrive!

You're Invited...

. . .to join us for any of our Sought After Speaker Summits!

Do you have a message you want to share?
Are you ready to improve your speaking skills?
Have you seen how much influence people who speak have?
Would you like be a sought-after speaker?

In one weekend you can develop your public speaking skills and be loud and proud about the value you bring. Join us for our next live event at: www.soughtafterspeaker.com

Because you are savvy enough to pick up this book we have a gift for you. Enter coupon code SASVIP50 for a 50% discount on your registration. Attend this event and watch how your social status climbs!

Get Published With Thrive Publishing™

THRIVE Publishing™ develops books for experts who want to share their knowledge with more and more people. We provide our co-authors with a proven system, professional guidance and support, thereby producing quality, multi-author how-to books that uplift and enhance the personal and professional lives of the people they serve.

We know that getting a book written and published is a huge undertaking. To make that process as easy as possible, we have an experienced team with the resources and know-how to put a quality, informative book in the hands of our co-authors quickly and affordably. Our co-authors are proud to be included in THRIVE Publishing™ books because these publications enhance their business missions, give them a professional outreach tool and enable them to communicate essential information to a wider audience.

You can find out more about our upcoming book projects at
www.thrivebooks.com.

Contact us to discuss how we can work together
on *your* book project.

Phone: **415-668-4535**
email: **info@thrivebooks.com**

Also from
THRIVE Publishing

For more information on
Direct Selling Power, visit:
www.thrivebooks.com/store

Also from
THRIVE Publishing

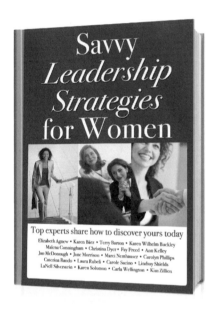

For more information on
Savvy Leadership Strategies for Women, visit:
www.thrivebooks.com/store

Also from
THRIVE Publishing

For more information on
Make Your Connections Count, visit:
www.thrivebooks.com/store

Also from
THRIVE Publishing

For more information on
Woman Entrepreneur Extraordinaire, visit:
www.thrivebooks.com/store

Also from
THRIVE Publishing

For more information on
Mom Entrepreneur Extraordinaire, visit:
www.thrivebooks.com/store

Also from
THRIVE Publishing

For more information on
Socially Smart & Savvy, visit:
www.thrivebooks.com/store

For more copies of this book,
A View From the Top Volume 3:
Avon's elite leaders share their stories
and strategies to succeed
contact any of the co-authors or visit
www.thrivebooks.com/store